Priceless

A DEVOTIONAL COOKBOOK

Based on Proverbs 31

Vickie Burns

REDEMPTION
PRESS

Published by Redemption Press, PO Box 427, Enumclaw, WA 98022.

Toll-Free (844) 2REDEEM (273-3336)

Redemption Press is honored to present this title in partnership with the author. The views expressed or implied in this work are those of the author. Redemption Press provides our imprint seal representing design excellence, creative content, and high-quality production.

The author has tried to recreate events, locales, and conversations from her memories of them. In order to maintain their anonymity, in some instances she has changed the names of individuals and may have changed some identifying characteristics and details, such as physical properties, occupations, and places of residence.

ISBN 13: 978-1-68314-947-7 (Paperback), 978-1-68314-948-4 (ePub), 978-1-68314-949-1 (Mobi)

Library of Congress Catalog Card Number: 2019907671

Priceless!

I have prayed specifically and intentionally for you while preparing and planning this project. The journey has been a long one, beginning several years ago. Through many adjustments and revisions, God remained faithful to guide me. He did a great work in getting this message into your hands. The message: You are priceless! This book is not only for you, it is about you. God made you in His image. He knew you before the foundation of the world. He gives you value. Your value was and is found in the cross of Christ. His resurrection made it possible for you to live out your days in abundant joy and priceless peace. My prayer is that you are blessed as much as I have been in completing this book. I pray that it will bless you as a woman, as a child of God, and as the bride of Christ.

Contents

Not Just Another
Ordinary Book on Your Shelf

*A*s you read or flip through this book, you will find that what you hold in your hands is not a typical devotional book, nor is it a customary cookbook. You will notice key differences immediately. First, each day is set up with a one-page devotional thought based on Proverbs 31. Second, you will find six questions that will help you reflect upon and apply the lessons found in the Scripture for the day. As you turn the page, the seventh question or activity is a prayer/journal page where you can respond to the prompt provided or simply record your thoughts. And lastly, you will find a menu for your evening meal. I have supplied a group of recipes (meals) that correspond with the week's theme in Scripture. For example, week one is about a mother's love. Therefore, week one's recipes are those you can teach to your sons/daughters. Week two is about the relationship between husband and wife, so the menus are all date-night-type meals. This pattern continues throughout the book, including meals for busy working moms, family favorites that can be shared during movie or game nights, and girly-girl-type meals to be enjoyed with your besties. While hospitality is far more than good food, one of the best times to share our hearts with others is while breaking bread together.

Heart of
Hospitality
VB

The Heart of Hospitality

As you will learn in our study, the heart of hospitality includes far more than a clean house and a good meal. It goes deeper than opening your home to guests. Hospitality is touching someone else's heart with a piece of your own. God shows us His hospitality every day in a variety of ways. His example inspires us to do the same.

At the end of each week, you will find a Weekend Wrap-Up where you can review the principles of hospitality that were covered during the study. Tear out these pages and place them in a prominent place in your home or office to inspire you to action as you share God's heart of hospitality with others. Use the verses listed with each principle to fill in the blanks. The answers are also found in the content of each day's devotion and activities.

Before turning another page, pray that God will use this study to draw you closer to Him, your family, your friends, and to people whom you have yet to meet. Ask Him to show you how much He loves and values you. Declare to the enemy that you will not believe his lies and that he is powerless to defeat the *priceless* blood of Christ that is within you.

My Prayer for This Study

Abba Father, bless the one holding this book right now, in the name of Jesus. May the words printed here lead to hope, joy, and peace in the hearts and lives of the reader, those in her household, and those in her church and community. Thank you, Daddy, for Your Word. I pray You bring it to life as hearts and homes are opened and shared in Your marvelous name.

Amen.

An excellent wife who can find?
She is far more precious than jewels.

Introduction

The key verse for this book and our time together is Proverbs 31:10: "An excellent wife who can find? She is far more precious than jewels."

More precious than jewels? What in this world could be more precious than pearls, diamonds, rubies, emeralds? The answer is simple: you! You are priceless. Something that is valued as priceless is rare, unique, and has significant meaning to its owner. As you read through the following statements, consider and rest in these truths:

Women who fear the Lord are hard to find. As one who seeks to honor God in her words and actions, you are rare. Your family, church, and community are blessed to have you and to have you serving them.

We are all created in the image of God, yet you have qualities that make you who you are. Not only do you have unique DNA and fingerprints, God gave you specific passions, gifts, talents, skills, and circumstances that He uses to bless His world when you seek to be used by Him. This makes you precious to your Creator and to those you serve.

Lastly, you have significant meaning to your Creator, your heavenly Daddy, your God. Your story began before the foundation of the world. God has known and loved you since before your parents knew one another. He has plans for you. He has a purpose for you. He has power to strengthen you through His Spirit in your inner being (Ephesians 3:16), all of which comes from His heart of love for you.

This week and in the weeks to come you will see that the virtuous woman described in Scripture is priceless because she is rare, unique, and has significant meaning to God and to her family. My prayer is that during your next few weeks of study and reflection you come to see yourself as priceless.

Background

The word "proverb" means "to be like." In the book of Proverbs, Solomon compares common, concrete images and life's most profound truths. Chapter 31 is no exception. The chapter consists of two poems that were taught to King Lemuel by his mother. According to ancient Jewish tradition, King Lemuel had been identified as King Solomon. If that was the case, his mother was Bathsheba. This puts an interesting spin on the chapter when we look through her eyes at Solomon and who she wants him to become, as well as the type of bride she wants for her son.

The first of the two poems is about a wise king, and the second is about a virtuous wife, both of which are rare and difficult to find. However, by the grace of God, they exist.

In this study we will discuss motherhood and the advice that we give our children. However, we will spend the bulk of our study identifying the priceless woman within, while learning some delicious recipes that will bring love, joy, and comfort into our homes.

If you are single or do not have children, the message in this book is for you as well. We all have people in our lives who look up to us as mothers or mentors. You may not be married now, but you might be one day, and no doubt you have close friends whom you love dearly. So in the place of wives and/or mothers, answer the questions as friends, sisters, aunts, and mentors. My prayer is that you, too, will be blessed.

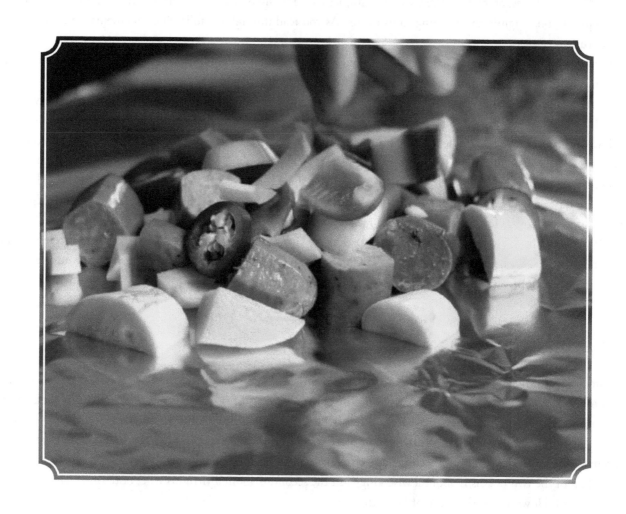

Sausage and Veggie Bake, page 20

A Mother's Love

Proverbs 31 is divided into two sections. The first contains words from a mother to her son King Lemuel. This week we will look at the initial nine verses and what this loving mother had to say to her son. These words were not merely prescriptive for King Lemuel, but they ring true for us as mothers of sons and daughters who will one day become husbands and wives and fathers and mothers. We will discuss and reflect on what kinds of advice we should give and the examples we should be for our children or those who look up to us. Because the lives we live in front of others show what we believe to be true about God, we must be intentional in our walk and our talk. As we touch the lives of those inside our homes, we have the potential to encourage and empower or frustrate and provoke. May we choose to build up and never tear down.

One of the best places to love your family well is sitting around the dinner table. To teach your children that food doesn't magically appear there, invite them to join in the preparation. The recipes this week are great for you to teach to your sons and daughters. They are quite versatile and have a range of complexity. If your children know how to cook these meals before they leave home to begin their adult lives, they will have a good grasp on a variety of cooking strategies that will impress any future spouse. I encourage you not to just let them watch but to engage your children in the process. Let them help. Give them a task and let them learn. Some of my most priceless memories of growing up were our times in the kitchen preparing and cleaning up after meals. I pray you have a similar experience.

Abba Father, guide me in truth this week regarding my words and actions. Let the words of my mouth and the meditation of my heart be pleasing in Your sight, O Lord. Let no hurtful words come from my mouth but only what is good for building up my children, friends, family, and acquaintances.

In Jesus's Name I Pray, Amen.

Like the love of our great God,
a mother's love is
unconditional and steadfast.

Motherly Advice

> The words of King Lemuel. An oracle that his mother taught him.
>
> Proverbs 31:1

AN ORACLE IS A PROPHECY OR A FORESHADOWING. THE HEBREW WORD USED IN THIS TEXT IS massâ (mas-saw). It means burden or mental desire. In the Old Testament God used prophets by giving them a burden, a mental desire, and a message to take to His people. The message we will be studying during the next few weeks is exactly that, a message from a mother to her son that reflects her burden and mental desire for his success in life.

If you are a mother, you know that the burden we have for our children to do well can be heavy. We do our best to lead them and teach them, and then we set them free. If you are not a mother, perhaps you have friends, nieces, or nephews whom you have mentored and led by example and encouragement. Regardless of who is placed in your charge, you long to provide them with words of wisdom. This is what we will find in this last chapter of Proverbs.

Knowing that we are to lead well by exemplifying God's commands and promises, what advice should we share? We see a mother warning her son of the temptations that come from being a man and a king. She addresses both the good that he should do and the bad that he should not. After verse nine we read another poem, one that was taught to the young king, which describes an excellent wife. This poem tells of the type of wife the mother wants for her son, the type of woman, wife, mother we strive to be. That advice is not always easy to give, nor is it easy to hear, even when spoken in love. We understand this truth when we realize that God's Word, though difficult to take at times, was given to us in love.

Like the love of our great God, a mother's love is unconditional and steadfast. God put that love in our hearts by giving His unwavering love to us. We will examine these words in light of Proverbs 31 and try to wrap our heads around what they mean for us today.

Reflection and Application

1. What is the best advice you have ever received?

2. What loving advice do you feel God has for you that might empower you to be a better example to your children or those around you?

3. Whom do you love unconditionally? How do they know it?

4. What words of wisdom or encouragement do you need to share with your children in their current stage of life? If you do not have children, how can you encourage someone who needs a kind word?

5. Define "unconditional love" in your own words. Find a verse that speaks of God's unconditional love for you and write it below.

6. Read Ephesians 4:29. During the next few days, pay close attention to the words that you say. Make notes below. Do your words build up or tear down?

Prayer / Journal

When was the last time you had a burden for a lost soul, a mental desire to help someone in need, or an important message to share with a loved one? God wants to speak to you and through you to deliver His message to others. Are you available? Ask Him now to give you a mental desire to share His Word, His love, His blessings with someone in your path today as you speak the truth in love. Record your prayer below.

_____

_____

_____

_____

_____

_____

_____

_____

_____

_____

_____

_____

_____

_____

_____

_____

_____

_____

_____

_____

Today's Meal
Spaghetti, Garlic Bread, Italian Salad

In the spirit of this week's message, here is something to teach to your children. This is the first meal I ever made for my family. I was seven years old and used jar sauce. I've made some significant changes to the recipe since then. It is simple to make and easy to teach your children so that they can cook for themselves or for their families. I hope you like it.

SPAGHETTI WITH MEAT SAUCE

1 lb. ground meat
1 can Italian stewed tomatoes
1 sm. onion (chopped)
1 sm. can tomato sauce
1 t. pepper
2 t. garlic salt (divided)
2 T. Italian seasoning (divided)

Brown ground meat with 1 teaspoon garlic salt, 1 tablespoon Italian seasoning, and onion. Drain if necessary.

To your meat add Italian tomatoes (blended if desired), tomato sauce, 1 tablespoon Italian seasoning and 1 teaspoon garlic salt. Add additional spices to taste.

Simmer 5–10 minutes.

Serve over your choice of pasta.

Note: Pulsing tomatoes in a blender helps hide them from picky eaters.

GARLIC BREAD

1 loaf of fresh french bread
½–1 stick of butter (softened)
Garlic salt
Parmesan cheese (optional)

Place loaf of bread on a cookie sheet. Slice bread into ¼–½ inch slices. Spread each slice with butter, keeping the loaf together as much as possible. Sprinkle each slice with garlic salt and parmesan. Put the loaf back together and cover with foil. Bake at 350° for 8–10 minutes or until butter is melted and bread is warmed through.

ITALIAN SALAD

Place your favorites of the following ingredients in a large bowl and toss with Olive Garden's (or your favorite) Italian dressing: iceberg and romaine lettuce, diced tomatoes, black olives, red onion (sliced), pepperoncini peppers, croutons, grated parmesan, and ground black pepper.

What Are You Doing?

What are you doing, my son? What are you doing, son of my womb?
What are you doing, son of my vows?

Proverbs 31:2

HAVE YOU EVER LOOKED AT YOUR CHILD AND ASKED THESE QUESTIONS: "WHAT ARE YOU DO-ing? What were you thinking? Did I not give birth to you? Are you the child I vowed to raise to honor God?" I know there are times in parenting when we all question the actions and thoughts of our children. It is in these times that we must take a deep breath, fall on our knees, and ask God for guidance, wisdom, and grace. Let Him give you the words and next steps to lead your child in making good choices. Ask God to help you respond in love rather than reacting in anger.

Now, let's put the shoe on the other foot. How many times has God looked at us and said, "What are you doing? What were you thinking? Did I not create you and am I not training you to live a life that honors Me? Have I not given you every reason to trust me?"

Did I just hear you say "Ouch!"?

When we stop and draw these parallel lines between God's direction in our imperfect lives and our parenting children who are not perfect, we can see how necessary it is for us to understand God's grace. God gives to us abundantly. We need to learn from the Master and extend grace to our children. John 1:16: "We have all received grace upon grace."

In the lives of our children, many times we search for the right words to say. We long to communicate grace and love in such a way that it "sticks." So when looking at this verse, imagine a mother trying to put just the right words together as she sends her son away to begin life on his own. She calls him "son of my vows." Much like Hannah in the book of 1 Samuel, this child was dedicated to the Lord. Both mothers loved their sons unconditionally. Both mothers wanted nothing more than to see their child grow up to honor and glorify Yahweh. Both mothers and sons needed grace to make this happen. Both mothers and children need grace throughout the growing-up process today.

Reflection and Application

1. In what areas of your life might God be asking "What are you doing?"

2. How would you answer?

3. Are there areas in your parenting where God's grace is needed?

4. Read 1 Samuel 1:1–8. What was Hannah's problem?

5. Read 1 Samuel 1:9–18. Describe the events in your own words.

6. Read and rejoice over 1 Samuel 1:19–28. What did you learn? How did God provide in obvious ways and not so obvious ways?

Prayer / Journal

Thank God today for the joy and responsibility of parenting children, mentoring protégées, and leading others. Thank Him for His direction in your life through those who have influenced you. Ask Him for the opportunity to influence others in their pursuit of Christ. We all have people we can come alongside and mentor. Ask God to reveal them to you today.

_____

_____

_____

_____

_____

_____

_____

_____

_____

_____

_____

_____

_____

_____

_____

_____

_____

_____

Today's Meal
Louisiana Hot Wings, Bacon Cheese Fries, Sweet Crunchy Coleslaw

This is my picky daughter's favorite! It is on the menu almost every month. Enjoy!

LOUISIANA HOT WINGS

1 3-lb. pkg. chicken wing sections
Peanut oil (frying oil of your preference)
¼ c. Original Louisiana hot sauce
¼ c. soy sauce
1 stick butter

Make sure wings are completely thawed and dry. Heat oil to 350˚. Fry wings in batches based on the size of your frying pan or cooker (be careful not to overfill), for about 7 minutes or until skin starts to tighten and pull away. As the first batch fries, melt butter in a large bowl and add sauces. As soon as wings are pulled from oil, toss in sauce mixture. Make sure all wings are well coated. Remove from sauce and place wings on a cookie sheet. Keep in a warm oven until all wings are ready. Reserve sauce for dipping. Keep lots of napkins handy.

For an extra kick, add a sprinkle of cayenne to your sauce.

Variations: Substitute soy and hot sauce with BBQ sauce or any variety wing sauce
Dipping: BBQ sauce, extra wing sauce, ranch dressing, blue cheese dressing, ketchup

SWEET CRUNCHY COLESLAW

Slaw:
½ head of cabbage (chopped)
1 sm. granny smith apple (diced small)
2–3 T. sugar
¾ c. slivered almonds
¾ c. parmesan cheese

Dressing:
⅓ c. sugar
1 t. salt
⅓ c. vinegar
⅔ c. canola oil

Prepare almonds: Place almonds and sugar in a saucepan. Stir constantly over medium heat until sugar melts and almonds are golden brown. Pour onto waxed paper or foil to cool.

Mix all other slaw ingredients in a large bowl and add almonds.

Whisk dressing ingredients together and pour over slaw.

Chill mixture for 20 minutes.

Another option: Instead of coleslaw, serve wings with spinach dip and Hawaiian bread. The recipe is on the package of Knorr vegetable dip mix.

For Bacon Cheese Fries: Fry frozen fries until crispy, arrange on a cookie sheet, sprinkle with shredded cheddar cheese, crispy crumbled bacon, and jalapenos (optional). Bake at 400° until cheese is melted.

Lay Down Your Idols

KING LEMUEL'S MOTHER ADVISED HIM TO BE CAREFUL NOT TO GIVE HIS STRENGTH AWAY TO women or his ways to those who destroy kings. We need to hear this lesson and heed this warning. When our top priority is anything other than our relationship with our Lord, we are giving our strength over to things, other people, and/or our passions.

The dictionary defines an idol as an image used as an object of worship; a false god; one that is adored, often blindly or excessively. The Bible says, "You shall have no other gods before Me" (Exodus 20:3).

We may not have any carved images in our homes or worship a deity other than the one true God, but what do we, as women, tend to put before God? Our homes? Our children? Our work? A body image we wish we had? A goal or dream? While none of these things are wrong or evil, they can each become our focus or, in many cases, an idol. When anything other than God becomes first in our lives, it will drain our energy, destroy our witness, and eventually break our hearts. Only our steadfast faith in God can strengthen us in our daily lives and give us true peace.

God does not ask for your allegiance out of obligation or service. God wants us to worship Him out of love: love for who He is, what He has done for you, and for His promises to lead you and never forsake you. His commandments:

> Teacher, which is the greatest commandment in the Law? And he said to him, "You shall love the Lord your God with all your heart and with all your soul and with all your mind. This is the great and first commandment." (Matthew 22:36–37)

> And the second is like it: you shall love your neighbor as yourself. (Matthew 22:38)

Reflection and Application

1. Make a list of your priorities today. What is your top priority?

2. Are there areas of your life that you need to turn over to God and allow Him to take control? List them below.

3. Look back at today's verse. What things, tasks, people tend to require most of your strength?

4. Look again at your list of priorities. Take out your planner, calendar, your phone, or a scratch piece of paper. On it, schedule 10–15 minutes alone with God each day, set a reminder, then plan the remainder of your day. Hint: Your time with God does not have to be at 4:30 in the morning, but if that works for you, schedule it!

5. List things that tend to be an idol for you: body image, perfect marriage, perfect home, money, success. Name them as your own.

6. Read 2 Samuel 11:1–12:25. What was David's idol? To what lengths did he go to get it and then to justify it? What did it cost him?

Prayer / Journal

Look at your idols and priorities again. Then mention each one by name as you pray and ask God to forgive any idolatry in your life. Pray these words to your heavenly Father as you write them below: *Search me, O God, and know my heart! Try me and know my thoughts, and see if there be any grievous way in me and lead me in the way everlasting.* (Psalm 139:23–24).

_____

_____

_____

_____

_____

_____

_____

_____

_____

_____

_____

_____

_____

_____

_____

_____

_____

_____

_____

_____

Today's Meal
Sausage and Veggie Bake, Grandma's Salad

This is a whole meal in a pouch. Use multiple pouches for each family member or one big one. Family members can decide what goes in their own pouch. Some may choose just meat and potatoes (that would be my daughter).

SAUSAGE AND VEGGIE BAKE

1 pkg. link sausage (we like polska kielbasa)
Your choice of veggies:
Cubed potatoes
Broccoli
Thick-cut squash
Thick-cut zucchini
Cubed onion
Cubed bell pepper
Brussel sprouts
Mushrooms
Fresh green beans
Whole garlic cloves
Olive oil
Roasted garlic-herb blend of spices (or your preference)

Prepare vegetables (except potatoes) by cutting into large pieces so they do not overcook. Cut potatoes into smallish cubes no bigger than an inch. Toss all vegetables in a large bowl with olive oil and spices (enough oil to thinly coat and enough spice to see some on each piece). Slice sausage into 2–3-inch pieces. Make a pouch with heavy-duty foil or purchase baking (grilling) pouches. Place all ingredients into foil pouches based on your preference. Bake in oven at 350° for 30 minutes or until potatoes are tender.

This works well when camping, cooked on a grill.

Variations: Use whole (skinless, boneless) chicken breasts or your favorite hearty fish. Season according to taste and place on the bottom of the pouch. Cover with vegetables and bake until chicken or fish is fully cooked.

Serve with: Green Salad or Grandma's Salad

GRANDMA'S SALAD

1 head iceberg lettuce (torn for salad)
2 med. tomatoes (diced)
1 can artichoke hearts (chopped)
2–3 avocados (diced)
3–4 T. dried onion flakes
Red wine vinegar
Extra virgin olive oil
Salt and pepper to taste

Combine vegetables and toss. Add onion flakes, olive oil, and vinegar, salt, and pepper to taste. Toss well and enjoy!

Too Much of a Good Thing

"It is not for kings, O Lemuel, it is not for kings to drink wine, or for rulers to take strong drink, lest they drink and forget what has been decreed and pervert the rights of all the afflicted. Give strong drink to the one who is perishing, and wine to those in bitter distress; let them drink and forget their poverty and remember their misery no more."

Proverbs 31:4–7

DON'T GET TOO EXCITED. I AM NOT GOING TO DEBATE WHETHER DRINKING IS WRONG OR permissible. What I am going to focus on is the lack of faith that causes us to do or consume anything in excess. In a sermon on gluttony, Paul Matthies defined it as "a lack of faith in God that expresses itself through excess and expects total satisfaction from some idol or choice at the expense of community, responsibility, and trusting worship of God" ("Defining Gluttony," The Village Church, Texas, November 5, 2006).

You may need to read that again slowly. I know I had to. Once you grasp what this says, the question is, what do you turn to in times of distress or frustration? What comfort do you seek when you are overwhelmed or depressed? What do you consume when no one is looking, or even when they are?

When we turn to things to fill a void and expect satisfaction, we run the risk of losing what is truly important in our lives. Our definition tells us that we could lose our sense of community—relationships with others suffer when we are not trusting God. We tend to use a crutch to avoid responsibilities and to isolate ourselves. But the most dangerous result can be that it keeps us from true and trusting worship of God.

There are times that we feel out of control. These can involve food, work, exercise, alcohol, success, or a whole realm of other things that we exchange for comfort, security, and happiness. Ladies, this is a scheme of the enemy to offer false, cheap imitations of pleasure that can and will impair our judgment. God alone is our source of comfort, security, and joy, and you can never have too much of Him! In order to embrace this, we must put our fleshly desires to death and seek first His kingdom and His righteousness (Matthew 6:33).

I have been crucified with Christ. It is no longer I who live, but
Christ who lives in me. And the life I now live in the flesh I live by
faith in the Son of God, who loved me and gave himself for me.
(Galatians 2:20)

21

Reflection and Application

1. Read John 4:23–24. Is gluttony or idolatry hindering your worship?

2. What areas of your life lead you to seek comfort in false imitations? Examples: work stress, wayward family members, finances, etc.

3. Read Luke 6:45. What is filling your heart? What comes out of your mouth when you face the anxieties you mentioned in question number 2?

4. On a scale of 1 to 10, how easy would it be for you to deny yourself that false imitation? Circle a number.

    1   2   3   4   5   6   7   8   9   10

5. Read Matthew 19:26. Using a different-colored pen or pencil, circle the number that represents how easy it would be for God to replace your false imitation with His comfort, security, and joy, and to fill the void in your life.

6. Name a person below to whom you can confess and ask for accountability in this area of weakness. Then write the date and time that you will have this discussion.

Prayer/Journal

Write your thoughts and prayers below. Ask God to bring the number you circled in number 4 up to the number you circled in number 5. Ask Him how to make that possible. Confess to Him your weakness and copy this verse in your prayer, replacing the pronouns with your name where applicable:

> But He (God) said to me (Vickie), "My grace is sufficient for you (Vickie), for My power is made perfect in weakness." Therefore I will boast all the more gladly of my weaknesses, so that the power of Christ may rest upon me.

Additionally, ask God for the boldness to speak to the friend who will help you and hold you accountable.

_____

_____

_____

_____

_____

_____

_____

_____

_____

_____

_____

_____

_____

_____

_____

_____

_____

_____

_____

_____

Today's Meal
Chicken Supreme, Sweet Green Beans, Garden Salad

Next to wings, this is my picky daughter's favorite. But don't put the veggies on hers. Just meat, bacon, and cheese. This is a crowd pleaser!

CHICKEN SUPREME

4–6 lg. chicken breasts, seasoned to taste
3–4 slices bacon
¼ med. onion
¼ sm. bell pepper
1 sm. can sliced mushrooms
1–1 ½ c. grated cheddar
1 pkg. angel hair pasta
Oil and salt
½ stick butter
2–3 cloves of garlic

Season chicken breasts (I use Tony's Cajun or Cavender's Greek). Add about 2 tablespoons of oil to a skillet and heat. When hot, add seasoned chicken breasts. Cook for 3 minutes on each side. Set aside chicken breasts. In large pot, cook angel hair pasta with a little oil and salt. When pasta is al dente, drain pot and toss pasta with melted butter and pressed garlic. Place pasta in 9x13-inch baking dish. Arrange chicken on top of pasta. In skillet, fry bacon and remove. In small amount of bacon drippings, sauté sliced veggies and mushrooms. Top chicken with broken bacon pieces and vegetables. Bake at 350° for 10–12 minutes (until chicken is fully cooked). Top with cheese and melt.

Variation: Use tenderized round steak instead of chicken. Season and place raw steak on cookie sheet. Top with cooked bacon and vegetables. Bake until meat is fully cooked. Top with cheese and melt. Serve with mashed potatoes instead of pasta.

SWEET GREEN BEANS

Variation: Using whole green beans, wrap bundles of 8–10 green beans with ½ slice of bacon. Place bundles in a sprayed baking dish, seam side down. Melt butter in a saucepan and whisk in sugar and garlic. Baste sauce onto bundles. Cover with foil and bake at 400° for 30 minutes. Uncover, baste, and bake for additional 10 minutes or until bacon is crispy.

6 slices of bacon cut into 1-inch pieces
¼ c. packed brown sugar
1 stick butter
1–2 T. garlic salt
1 lb. fresh or frozen cut green beans

In a medium saucepan, fry cut bacon. When bacon is almost crispy, add butter. When melted, add green beans and enough water to just cover. Add garlic salt and stir. Simmer on low until green beans are tender and have absorbed flavor.

Serve with: Rolls and salad

GARDEN SALAD

Mix together your preferred salad veggies and toppings—salad greens, carrots, cucumbers, radishes, tomatoes, broccoli, avocado, onions, peppers, etc. Add your favorite dressing.

20/20 Vision

Open your mouth for the mute, for the rights of all who are destitute.
Open your mouth, judge righteously; defend the rights of the poor and needy.

Proverbs 31:8–9

DO YOU SEE THEM? CAN YOU HEAR THEIR DESPERATE CRIES? CAN YOU FEEL THEIR PAIN? DO you understand their helplessness? Do you want to?

Personally, I am guilty of tunnel vision. I tend to have blinders on as I hurry through my day and work hard to complete all my tasks. I do not have time to help others with their problems. I have enough of my own. Wow, am I selfish!

When statistics show that poverty is on the rise and hunger is running rampant but we do not see it, does that mean it's not there? That hunger, poverty, pain, and suffering are simply not in our realm of influence? Chances are they are right under our noses and we are too wrapped up in ourselves to see them.

But maybe we do see them. What if we are fully aware of the needs around us? Do we just point fingers, thinking it is somehow their fault to be in the mess they are in or that others are supposed to make things right and meet their needs? Or, at the very least, do we pray for them? "Lord, protect and provide for those in need." In James 2:15–16, God's Word says:

> If a brother or sister is poorly clothed and lacking in daily food, and one of
> you says to them, "Go in peace, be warmed and filled," without giving them
> the things needed for the body, what good is that?

James goes on to say that our faith without works is dead. To be Christian is to be like Christ. While Jesus was on earth, in the flesh, He spent His years of ministry serving, speaking, healing, and helping all who came to Him and all He came across. He spoke up for those with no voice in society. He taught us by example as well as in words.

Reflection and Application

1. Are you aware of needs around you? Poverty? Grief? What are you doing to help?

2. When was the last time you helped someone with a need?

3. Have you ever spoken up for someone or a group of people who could not or would not speak for themselves? How did that go?

4. Look around at work and at church. Visit local shelters or local food pantries. Write the day and time that you will visit and volunteer to meet the needs of those in your community.

5. Read Matthew 25:31–46. What will you do "for the least of these"?

6. Listen to Brandon Heath's song "Give Me Your Eyes." Write the words of the song that speak to you the most.

Prayer/Journal

Pray, asking God to give you eyes and a heart for the hurting and needy around you. Ask Him to help you see them like He does. Confess your blindness to Him, and ask for perfect vision and a mouth to speak for those who cannot and/or do not.

_____

_____

_____

_____

_____

_____

_____

_____

_____

_____

_____

_____

_____

_____

_____

_____

_____

_____

_____

_____

_____

_____

Today's Meal
Chicken Fried Protein, Deluxe Mashed Potatoes, Gravy, Purple Hull Peas

Peas are great with cornbread, but fried foods with gravy are best with hot rolls. You decide! If you can teach your child to chicken fry protein, whether steak, chicken strips, or deer meat, you are gold!

CHICKEN FRIED PROTEIN

1–2 lb. protein (round steak, chicken breast, deer steak)
Spices (Tony's, Cavender's, salt and pepper)
2 c. flour
Salt
Pepper
1 egg
¾ c. milk
Oil for frying

Cut meat into serving-size portions, pound to ¼-inch thick and season to taste. Fill a large skillet or deep fat fryer about half full. Heat oil to 350˚. Combine flour, salt, and pepper on a plate or small dish with sides. In a separate bowl, whisk together eggs and milk. Dip each steak in milk mixture and then coat well with flour mixture. When oil is hot, carefully place meat in oil and fry until juices surface and coating is golden brown (about 2–3 minutes per side). Remove and drain on paper towel-lined platter.

DELUXE MASHED POTATOES

6–8 med. potatoes
Salt and pepper
1 stick butter
2 sm. shallots
2 cloves garlic
¼–½ c. heavy cream
Milk

Peel and wash potatoes. Dice or slice potatoes and place in a large boiling pot. Cover with water and add a dash of salt. Boil until tender. In a small saucepan, melt butter. Add thinly sliced shallots and minced garlic. Sauté until tender. Set aside. Drain potatoes and return to pot. Add butter combination and mash well (using mixer if desired). Add heavy cream and milk to desired texture. Salt and pepper to taste.

MMM GRAVY

With about 4 tablespoons of drippings from fried protein in a skillet, add 3 heaping tablespoons of flour. Whisk until blended and bubbly, over medium heat. Slowly add 1 ½ to 2 cups of milk. Whisk constantly until desired consistency. Add milk as needed for thinning. Salt and pepper to taste. Transfer to serving bowl.

PURPLE HULL OR FIELD PEAS

Cut 2–3 slices of bacon into 1-inch pieces and fry until almost crispy. Add a small bag of frozen peas and enough water to cover them. Bring to a rolling boil for 5 minutes. Add salt and pepper to taste (I also add a dash of Tony's Seasoning). Reduce heat to low and simmer until peas are tender, about 30 minutes. Peas will absorb water quickly. Check every 5 minutes and keep covered with water.

A Mother's Love
Weekend Wrap-Up

Using what you've learned this week and the verses listed with each statement, fill in the blanks to help you remember the truth regarding God's love for you and how we are to love others.

Hospitality 101: Understanding God's Love

- God first _____ us (1 John 4:19).

- God offers _____ upon _____ (John 1:16).

- God's love gives me _____ (Philippians 4:13).

- God _____ the void with _____ and _____ (Romans 15:13).

- God provides for our _____ (Matthew 6:25–32).

Hospitality 102: Loving Others

- We should speak the _____ in love (Ephesians 4:15–16).

- We are called to extend _____ as it is given to us (2 Corinthians 4:13–15).

- Strength to _____ others comes from the love of God (1 John 4:11).

- We need to seek first the _____ of God and His _____ (Matthew 6:33).

- Love through _____ of faith (James 2:15–18).

My thoughts concerning this week's study:

_____

_____

_____

_____

_____

_____

_____

_____

_____

_____

_____

_____

_____

_____

_____

_____

_____

_____

_____

_____

_____

_____

Weekend Wrap-Up Desserts

CHOCOLATE PIE

1 Pillsbury pie crust
1 ¼ c. milk
1 ½ c. sugar
4 egg yolks
3 T. cocoa (heaping)
1 t. vanilla
4 T. flour (heaping)
4 T. butter

Meringue
4 egg whites
½ t. vanilla
½ t. cream of tartar
¾ c. sugar

Bake pie crust according to package directions. In a microwavable mixing bowl, combine 1 ½ cups sugar, cocoa, and flour. Use the backside of a large spoon to press out all the lumps. Make sure mixture is well combined and smooth. Add milk and egg yolks. Whisk thoroughly. Add butter (no need to melt first). Place bowl in microwave. Cook for 3 minutes. Remove and whisk again. Microwave 3 minutes. Remove, add vanilla, and whisk again. Microwave 2 minutes longer. Remove, whisk, and pour into baked pie crust.

While filling is cooling, beat egg whites and cream of tartar until foamy. Add vanilla and continue beating while slowly adding sugar, one tablespoon at a time. Beat until soft peaks form.

Top pie filling with meringue, being sure to press meringue all the way to the crust, making soft peaks.

Bake in 350° oven until peaks are golden brown.

Almond Joy Pie: After the first time in the microwave, add ½ cup sweetened coconut and ¼ cup sliced almonds. After topping with meringue, sprinkle a little coconut, cocoa powder, and a few almonds on top of meringue before browning in the oven.

Coconut Pie: Use the same recipe above, omitting cocoa powder and adding 1 cup coconut. Top meringue with coconut before browning in the oven.

CHOCOLATE CHIP COOKIES

¾ c. butter-flavored Crisco
1 ¼ c. flour
¾ c. brown sugar
1 sm. pkg. instant vanilla pudding
¾ c. white sugar
1 t. salt
2 T. milk
¾ t. baking soda
1 T. vanilla
1 c. semisweet chocolate chips
1 egg
1 c. pecans, chopped

Cream Crisco, sugars, milk, and vanilla in a large bowl with a mixer. Blend in egg. In a small bowl, combine dry ingredients (flour, dry pudding, salt, baking soda). Slowly add and blend into creamed mixture. Stir in chocolate chips and nuts. Drop rounded scoops of dough onto ungreased cookie sheet (2–3 inches apart). Bake at 350° for 8–10 minutes (until cookies have just lost their shiny wet appearance).

Shrimp Tacos, page 46

An Excellent Wife

my prayer is that this week will be relevant and helpful to you whether you are married or single. I pray you will learn that working hard and resting easy is only possible through Christ. "For 'in Him we live and move and have our being'; as even some of your own poets have said, 'for we are indeed His offspring'" (Acts 17:28).

Through His love and mercy, we can and should do all things in the name of the Lord Jesus (Colossians 3:17).

All the things you do matter. These things are important to you, to your family, and to your God. He made each of us with special qualities and skills, abilities and passions. These qualities align perfectly with your personal ministry to your family and community. God has put you where you are for a reason. He has given you a piece of Himself as He made you in His image. This piece is meant to be shared with those He places in your life. As you share, you are showing hospitality as it is meant to be. Sharing your unique talents, skills, and gifts as a blessing to others makes you *priceless*. You are priceless to God as His daughter. You are priceless to others as their mother, wife, sister, friend, and coworker. You are priceless when you can look in the mirror and see the beauty of God's creation.

I pray God will show you that you are priceless and worthy of love. I can't wait for you to see and believe that you are priceless in Christ. This can and will change the way you see yourself, and ultimately the way you serve others.

Serving your significant other will be made easy this week, at least in the way of mealtime. Since the verses and content we will cover relate mostly to husband and wife, our menus will follow suit. Your date-night meals are designed for two. Enjoy them with your husband, your date for the evening, or your best friend. However, these are usually favorites of the whole family, so feel free to increase the quantity to share with your family and friends.

Father, reveal Yourself to me this week. Teach me how to live in the identity You have given me. Help me believe that I am known and loved. Provide opportunities for me to share Your love with others so that they know they are priceless.

In Your Priceless Name, Amen.

You are priceless
when you can
look in the mirror
and see the beauty
of God's creation.

An Excellent Wife

An excellent wife who can find? She is far more precious than jewels.

Proverbs 31:10

EXCELLENCE. IT IS SOMETHING WE STRIVE FOR, YET IT SEEMS TO BE JUST OUT OF REACH. THE word "excellent" has been defined as possessing outstanding quality or superior merit; remarkably good.

This definition has the potential to make us feel inadequate. In fact, the rest of this chapter could make any one of us want to throw up our hands and call it quits as we perceive that we may never live up to the standard. This is exactly where the enemy wants us. Satan can and will make us question our worth, even and especially when we are studying God's Word. The enemy likes it when we get down on ourselves, when we question the way God created us, and when we doubt our value and purpose in life. He hates it when we study and learn the truth about ourselves in God's Word. So he does what he can to twist it.

Stand firm, my sister! You are fearfully and wonderfully made (Psalm 139:14–15) in the image and likeness of the one true God (Genesis 1:26–31). You are excellent by design. The design is flawless because He is flawless.

So why is excellence so hard to find? After all, no one has ever been walking along and just stumbled upon a rare jewel. Jewels take time and multiple processes to uncover. By comparison, you too are a precious jewel undergoing the process of refinement.

2 Corinthians 3:18 says:

> And we all, with unveiled faces, beholding the glory of the Lord, are
> being transformed into the same image from one degree of glory to
> another. For this comes from the Lord, who is the Spirit.

Inside each of us is the Spirit of God. We must allow Him to work in us and shine through us. He is our excellence! When we walk not according to the flesh but according to the Spirit (Romans 8:11), the world will see His excellence. That's what makes us priceless.

Reflection and Application

1.   Only through God's grace and the help of the Holy Spirit can we become the excellent wife, mother, friend, sister, and child of the King! What does this statement mean to you?

2.   Read Psalm 139:13–16. Write your thoughts regarding this passage below.

3.   When you look in a mirror, do you see excellence? Why or why not?

4.   Read James 1:23–25. When you look in the mirror of God's Word, do you see excellence? Why or why not?

5.   Look up the definition of "excellent." Make a list of everything that is excellent about you and your life.

6.   Write Psalm 139:14 on an index card, replacing the personal pronouns with your name. Tape it to the mirror you use every day (the mirror that you used to answer number 3 above).

Prayer / Journal

The God of the universe, the great I Am, is excellent! He loves you. He lives inside of you. Pray and ask Him to reveal Himself to you. Ask Him to help you see yourself the way He does. Ask Him to reveal Himself to others through you. Excellence doesn't have to be hard to find.

_____

_____

_____

_____

_____

_____

_____

_____

_____

_____

_____

_____

_____

_____

_____

_____

_____

_____

_____

_____

Today's Meal
Steak, Baked-Potato Volcanos, Bacon-Wrapped Asparagus, Strawberry Spinach Salad

The meals for this week are for couples, as the verses we will cover are for husbands and wives. Feel free to serve as many as you want for ordinary days or special occasions.

GRILLED STEAK

2 steaks of your choice
Montreal steak seasoning (or your choice of spices)
Unflavored cooking spray

Bring steaks to room temperature. Lightly spray both sides of your steaks with cooking spray and sprinkle generously with steak seasoning. Place steaks on hot grill. Grill each side to desired color. Use a digital meat thermometer to determine doneness. Rare, 120°–125°; medium rare, 130°–135°; well done, 155°.

Important: Let meat rest for about 5 minutes before cutting. This allows the temp to regulate and for juices to redistribute themselves.

BACON-WRAPPED ASPARAGUS

Break off woody ends of each spear. Coat asparagus with olive oil and sprinkle with steak seasoning. Wrap 4–6 spears with a slice of bacon. Bake bundles at 400° for 15 minutes or until bacon is fully cooked.

BAKED-POTATO VOLCANOS

2 lg. baking potatoes
Extra virgin olive oil
Coarse salt
2–4 slices of bacon
Potato toppings: cheese, sour cream, butter, chives, salt, pepper
2 slices cheddar cheese (folded into fourths)

Coat potatoes with olive oil and sprinkle with salt. Bake on a baking sheet at 375° until tender when squeezed (about an hour). Cut the rounded ends off each end of potatoes. With a small spoon, scoop out the center of the potato into a medium mixing bowl, leaving about ¾ inch in the bottom. Add your desired toppings to the bowl and mix well. Carefully refill potatoes with mixture. Wrap each potato with strips of bacon and secure with toothpicks. Place on cookie sheet and bake at 350° for 15–20 minutes until bacon is done. Top with folded cheddar cheese slice and return to oven until cheese is melted and running down the side of the potato.

STRAWBERRY SPINACH SALAD

In a large mixing bowl, mix together 1 bag of baby spinach, ½ cup of grapes (halved), ¼ cup bacon bits, 1 small carton of strawberries (sliced). Dressing: ½ cup oil, ⅛ cup red wine vinegar, ¼ cup sugar, ½ teaspoon salt, ½ teaspoon Worcestershire sauce, ¼ cup minced red onion. Drizzle dressing over salad.

Priceless

An excellent wife who can find? She is far more precious than jewels.

Proverbs 31:10

THIS VERSE REMINDS ME OF THE OLD COMMERCIALS FOR MASTERCARD THAT WOULD TELL A story through the purchase of something that was ultimately priceless. Depending on the version of your Bible, yours may compare the excellent wife to pearls, diamonds, or rubies. So picture this:

She has a diamond on her finger: $3,500
Her neck is adorned with rubies: $1,000
Pearls dangle from her ears: $500
A woman who fears the Lord: Priceless

You are worth more than the finest gold, silver, and jewels. A woman who fears the Lord is to be praised. Why? Because of her unique qualities. Much like rare gems, women who fear the Lord are rare and have fine qualities that make her stand out above others. Her heart is pure. She is lovely. Her friends find her trustworthy and wise.

There may be times when you think you hear the woman in this chapter say the old familiar line from the L'Oréal commercial, "Don't hate me because I'm beautiful." Listen again. This woman is beautiful, but she is also humble and godly. She would never look down upon anyone, nor would she build herself up.

Today I want you to understand that you are this woman. You are priceless. Your heart is pure in the eyes of the Lord if you belong to Him. You are lovely, trustworthy, and wise through the power of the Spirit working in your inner being. Will we make mistakes? Yes! But there is therefore now no condemnation for those who are in Christ Jesus (Romans 8:1).

Reflection and Application

1. Do you see yourself as priceless? Why or why not? (This is not the same question from yesterday.)

2. Look up these jewels and gems on the internet and fill in the chart below. I did the first one for you. Google works best—it doesn't have to be exact.

	Pearl	Ruby	Diamond	
Value	$300 to $1500			
Rarity	extremely			
Symbolism	Purity, generosity, integrity			

3. Look up the following verses and match them to the purposes and plans for which you were created.

    _____ Psalms 4:3   A . . . a vessel for honorable use . . .
    _____ 2 Timothy 2:21   B . . . the Lord looks at the heart . . .
    _____ 2 Corinthians 5:20   C . . . set apart the godly for Himself . . .
    _____ 1 Samuel 16:7   D . . . we are ambassadors for Christ . . .

4. In the heading for the last column, write your name. What would you say about your value? Write it on the chart.

5. What would you say about your rarity? Write it on the chart.

6. What would you say about your purpose? Write it on the chart.

Prayer/Journal

You are beautiful. You are rare. You were bought with a price. You are His! Write a prayer below asking God to reveal who you really are in Him. Thank Him for making you priceless. Thank Him for making you flawless in His sight.

_____

_____

_____

_____

_____

_____

_____

_____

_____

_____

_____

_____

_____

_____

_____

_____

_____

_____

_____

_____

_____

Today's Meal
Chicken Parmesan, Italian Salad, Garlic Buttered Bread Sticks

CHICKEN PAREMSAN

1 12-oz. package uncooked spaghetti
4 boneless, skinless chicken breast halves
1 lg. egg (beaten)
Salt and pepper
¾ c. Italian bread crumbs
4 T. butter
1 14-oz. jar favorite spaghetti sauce
¾ c. mozzarella cheese (grated)
¼ c. chopped fresh parsley
Parmesan for garnish (freshly grated is best)

Cook pasta according to package directions. Lightly season chicken with salt and pepper. Place chicken between two sheets of heavy-duty plastic wrap and flatten with rolling pin to ¼-inch thickness. Dip chicken in egg. Remove and coat with breadcrumbs. Melt butter in skillet over medium heat. Add chicken and cook 8 minutes on each side until tender and no longer pink. Drain chicken on paper towel and set aside. Heat sauce in a medium saucepan, adding seasonings to taste (Italian seasoning and garlic salt if needed). Place drained spaghetti in 9x13-inch baking dish. Top with chicken. Pour sauce over chicken and top with grated mozzarella. Bake in 450° oven 5 minutes or until cheese is melted. Sprinkle with parmesan and parsley.

For Italian Salad: See page 12.

GARLIC BUTTERED BREAD STICKS

Pillsbury bread sticks
1 stick of butter
2 cloves of garlic
¼ teaspoon salt
½ teaspoon parsley

Lay bread sticks on cookie sheet. In a small skillet, melt butter, press garlic through garlic press or finely mince and add to butter. Add salt and parsley. Brush bread sticks with garlic butter and bake according to package directions. Serve extra garlic butter at the table for dipping.

His Heart

TRUST IS A FRAGILE THING. WE PUT OUR TRUST IN PEOPLE, OBJECTS, AND IDEALS. WHEN ANY one of these fails to do what we trust it to do, that trust is broken. We decide not to trust that "whatever" again. At the very least we find ourselves wary of putting all of our trust in it the next time. Because of its fragility, trust must be earned and re-earned when necessary.

Today's verse says the heart of her husband trusts her. Why do you think it specifically says his heart trusts her? To answer that question, let's look at what it means to trust with our heads versus trusting with our hearts. To say I trust that parachutes work and save lives is trust with my head. It is not until I jump from an airplane at an altitude of 12,500 feet and pull the rip cord that I am trusting with my heart that parachutes do what they are made to do.

So here's the question: Would your husband put his heart in your hands? Does he trust that you are forever faithful? Does he know that he is second in your life, coming only after your Lord and Savior? It might be interesting to ask him, if you are so bold. If these questions invoke fear or doubt, remember the woman who fears the Lord and keeps Him number one is worthy of her husband's wholehearted trust.

> The woman who fears the Lord and keeps Him number one is worthy of her husband's wholehearted trust.

The verse below is one of my life verses. I have personalized it by simply changing the pronouns. Read and reflect on the statement below based on Proverbs 3:5–6:

When I . . . trust in the Lord with all (my) heart and do not lean on (my) own understanding, [and] in all (my) ways (I) acknowledge Him, He will make straight (my) paths (and trustworthy my ways).

Reflection and Application

1. In what ways do you personally relate to today's message of rare, wholehearted trust?

2. What does it mean to you to trust with your heart versus trust with your head?

3. Whom do you trust with your heart?

4. Think about your conversations outside of your husband's (friend's) presence. How trustworthy are you to keep the hearts of others protected from slander, gossip, or the subject of a gripe session?

5. What do you need to do based upon your answer to number 4?

6. Read Ephesians 4:1–3. In your calling to be a wife, mother, or friend, which of the qualities listed in these verses is most likely to stand in the way of your being trustworthy?

Prayer / Journal

Take time to look back at your answers to the previous questions. Let this be a brief time of confession. Then take time for gladness and thanksgiving. Know that our God is trustworthy, and, since we are His image bearers, He can help us be the same.

_____

_____

_____

_____

_____

_____

_____

_____

_____

_____

_____

_____

_____

_____

_____

_____

_____

_____

_____

_____

_____

Today's Meal
Shrimp Tacos, Guacamole, Spanish Fried Rice

SHRIMP TACOS

6–8 corn tortillas
1 poblano pepper (sliced)
1 red bell pepper (sliced)
1 red onion (sliced)
3 T. butter plus 2 T. butter
1 lb. small shrimp (peeled)
Old Bay Seafood Seasoning
Tony's Cajun Seasoning

In a large skillet, melt 3 tablespoons butter. Add peppers and sauté on medium heat for 2 minutes. Add onion and sauté until all veggies are almost tender. Push veggies to edges of the pan. Melt 2 tablespoons butter in the center. Add shrimp to the center of the pan and sprinkle with spices (dust with a light coat of each). Toss shrimp until opaque. Set aside.

The best way to heat corn tortillas (that I have found) is to lightly spray one side with cooking spray and place it spray side down on a hot griddle. Spray the other side and heat both sides until barely toasty but still soft. Store on a paper towel between two plates or in a foil pouch.

Serve with sour cream if desired.

GUACAMOLE

2 lg. ripe avocados
¼ sm. onion (chopped small)
2 sm. Roma tomatoes (chopped small)
Salt
1 c. shredded lettuce

Mash avocados with onion and tomatoes. Add salt to taste. Add shredded lettuce and combine gently.

Serve with chips or on tacos.

SPANISH FRIED RICE

1 c. rice
2 T. oil
1 cube chicken bouillon
1 t. salt
¼ c. salsa
1 ¾ c. boiling water

In a medium saucepan stir rice and oil over medium heat until rice begins to be toasted. In a large measuring cup, dissolve bouillon cube and salt in boiling water. Add salsa. Slowly pour mixture into rice. Watch for steam! Bring to a boil. Cover, reduce heat to medium-low, and cook until all moisture is cooked from rice, about 10 minutes. Check at 7 minutes to determine if additional time is needed.

His Gain

The heart of her husband trusts her, and he will have no lack of gain.

Proverbs 31:11

THE PHRASE "NO LACK OF GAIN" IS THE SAME PHRASE FROM THE ORIGINAL ANCIENT TEXT USED in Psalm 23: "I shall not want." The Lord is our Shepherd and we have no need that He does not fill. In much the same way, in a household where the woman fears the Lord and seeks to honor her husband, he has no need that must be met outside the home. This woman is resourceful, wise, and talented. She is not lazy, nor is she an over-spender. Her husband does not work to replenish what she wastes, but rather labors to lavish upon her the love and trust that she deserves.

Her contribution to the marriage and their family supplements his and provides stability in the home. The woman who fears the Lord handles the affairs of her home in such a way that her husband need not worry. She seeks to honor God as her first priority, and in doing so, honors her husband and family. This provides both comfort and security for her husband.

Look again at the preceding paragraphs. Ask God for His perspective. Do not let your heart be troubled. God is on your side. Where we are weak, He is strong. Is living a life that honors God and our husbands easy? No! Certainly not in our own strength. But that is the bad news and the good news.

Jesus said in John 15:5:

> "I am the vine; you are the branches. Whoever abides in me and I
> in him, he it is that bears much fruit, for apart from me you can do
> nothing."

All we have to do is stay plugged in to our life source: the Vine. He does the impossible in us and through us. With Jesus as our source of strength and the author of our faith, our husbands and families will lack no good thing.

Reflection and Application

1. Based on John 15:5, what is your "abide" status on a scale of 1 to 10? What will it take to make your number higher?

2. Why isn't your number lower? In other words, what are you currently doing to abide?

3. List the fruit in your home that you have or want to have as a result of abiding in Christ.
   Fruit = Good things happening and/or being done in your home
   Qualities of that fruit = love, joy, peace, patience, kindness, goodness, faithfulness, gentleness, self-control

4. Take inventory. If you are brave, ask your husband if there is anything that he needs from you that you are not supplying. Be ready for the answer. Do not get defensive. Simply respond, "Thank you. I'll work on that with God's help." Write his answer below. If you are not quite ready to be so bold, ask yourself what needs he has that you need God's help to fulfill.

5. Read Psalm 23. List below the benefits of abiding in Him.

6. Read John 15:1–11. Write your reflections below. How hospitable is your heart toward God? Would He feel welcome there?

Prayer/Journal

In today's prayer, acknowledge God as your Shepherd. Thank Him for the benefits you listed in question number 5—make them personal to you. Ask God to help you abide in Him so that you can lovingly pursue the heart of your husband.

_____

_____

_____

_____

_____

_____

_____

_____

_____

_____

_____

_____

_____

_____

_____

_____

_____

_____

_____

_____

_____

_____

Today's Meal
Cajun Shrimp on Toast, Steamed Broccoli, Vegetable Medley

CAJUN SHRIMP ON TOAST

Sauce
½ stick butter
1 pt. heavy cream
½ lemon
3 T. Old Bay Seasoning
1 clove garlic (minced)
¼ sm. onion (minced)
3 T. mustard

Shrimp
1 lb. peeled small shrimp
1 clove garlic (minced)
2 t. salt
½ stick butter
1 t. red pepper flakes
½ t. oregano
¼ c. chicken broth or cooking wine

Bread
1 loaf french bread
Extra virgin olive oil

Assembly: Place one piece of toast on individual plate, spoon 10–12 shrimp on toast, drizzle with sauce.

For sauce: Melt butter in a saucepan over medium heat. Add minced onion and garlic. When vegetables are soft, squeeze lemon into pan (careful not to let seeds go). Add cream, mustard, and spices. Reduce to low heat and stir often. Do not allow sauce to boil.

For shrimp: Melt butter in small skillet over high heat. Add garlic, salt, and red pepper flakes. Whisk and add shrimp. Just before shrimp are done, add chicken broth or wine.

For bread: Slice bread into 1-inch slices and place on a cookie sheet. Drizzle with olive oil. Put under broiler until barely toasted. Turn bread over, drizzle with oil again, and toast other side.

VEGETABLE MEDLEY

2–3 slices bacon
1 can diced tomatoes and green chilies, drained
1 lg. yellow squash
1 lg. zucchini

Cut bacon into 1-inch pieces and fry in medium skillet over high heat. Drain grease and add bacon back to pan. Pour in drained diced tomatoes and green chilies and add vegetables. Simmer over medium heat until vegetables are tender, about 10 minutes.

STEAMED BROCCOLI

1 sm. head of broccoli
Salt and pepper to taste
Lemon juice (optional)

Place broccoli in steamer. Steam until desired texture, about 10 minutes. Sprinkle with spices and lemon juice if desired.

The Power of Words

THEY SAY THAT ACTIONS SPEAK LOUDER THAN WORDS. IN MANY WAYS, THIS IS TRUE. HOWEVER, our words are quite powerful. Our verse today says that we are to do our husbands good and not harm. I believe that this refers not only to our actions but also our words and attitudes.

What do you do for your husband that is good? How do you keep him from harm? Now the tough ones . . . What do you say to and about your husband that is good? Are your words (thoughts) sometimes harmful?

Ephesians 4:29 says:

> Let no corrupting talk come out of your mouths, but only such as is
> good for building up, as fits the occasion, that it may give grace to
> those who hear.

When are you most likely to struggle with your attitude, actions, and words? Oftentimes we catch ourselves in a vicious cycle of negativity. This happens when we are tired, stressed, hungry, or overwhelmed. We get down on ourselves, our children, our homes, our lives, and our husbands. That's when most of us open our hurting hearts and our mouths begin to express hurtful words. Satan wants nothing more than to drive a wedge into our homes in order to divide and conquer. He will use our words and actions as his weapons at every opportunity.

John 10:10 says, "The thief comes only to steal and kill and destroy." We must never allow the thief into our homes, our minds, or our hearts. When negativity creeps in, take authority. When arguments begin, stop and pray. When the enemy attacks, put him in his place! Then, remind your husband how much you love and adore him. Together you will have victory over the enemy.

Reflection and Application

1. "She does him good, and not harm, all the days of her life."

    How do you personally relate to the rare kind of love portrayed by this excellent wife from Proverb 31:12?

2. The verse today says, "She does him good and not harm." List the good you do for your husband and for others.

3. How and when does the enemy most often attack your marriage?

4. Read 2 Corinthians 10:3–6. List any strongholds, arguments, lofty opinions, and thoughts over which you need to take authority.

5. Read Philippians 2:3–4 in the Amplified Version of the Bible. What motives need to be present behind what you say and do for those in your home?

6. Read Philippians 4:8. How can you reverse the negative and turn your thoughts to positive when Satan tries to get you down?

Prayer / Journal

Sit with your husband and pray together today. Ask God to help you treat each other in such a way that God is honored. Take authority, in Jesus's name, over the enemy by listing your answers to numbers 3 and 4 and telling Satan that he cannot have any part of your thoughts, hearts, or lives!

_____

_____

_____

_____

_____

_____

_____

_____

_____

_____

_____

_____

_____

_____

_____

_____

_____

_____

_____

_____

Today's Meal
Poblano Chicken, Farfalle Pasta, Roasted Vegetables, Grandma's Salad

POBLANO CHICKEN

6 boneless chicken breasts
Salt and pepper or seasoning preference
2 lg. poblano peppers
2–3 T. extra virgin olive oil
½ c. milk
2 T. flour
1 stick butter
2 c. heavy cream
½ c. shredded cheese
12 oz. farfalle pasta

Preheat oven to 450°. Pound chicken breasts flat, season to taste. Rub peppers with olive oil and place on baking sheet. Roast for 5–7 minutes or until peppers blister. Remove skin, stem, and seeds. Reduce oven temp to 350°. Melt ½ stick butter in medium saucepan, add flour, and stir over medium heat. In a blender, puree 1 pepper in milk. Add pureed mixture to saucepan and whisk well. Add heavy cream. Cook over low heat until thick and bubbly. Add salt and pepper to taste. In a large skillet, melt other ½ stick of butter. Sear chicken for 3–4 minutes on each side. Place chicken in a baking dish. Slice other pepper and lay strips on top of chicken. Cover chicken with sauce and shredded cheese. Bake for 5 minutes.

Cook farfalle pasta according to directions on package. Serve chicken and sauce over pasta.

ROASTED VEGETABLES

10–12 new potatoes
1–2 yellow squash
1–2 zucchini
1 med. onion
1 pt. sliced mushrooms
Extra virgin olive oil
Roasted garlic spices (grinder)

Preheat oven to 400°. Dice all vegetables into large bite-sized pieces (they will shrink). In a small saucepan, bring potatoes to a boil. Turn off the burner and wait 3 minutes. Place all diced vegetables (including potatoes) in a large mixing bowl, drizzle with olive oil, and sprinkle with spices. Stir to make sure all veggies are coated. Pour veggies on a cookie sheet. Bake at 400° for 20–30 minutes, stirring and turning every 5 minutes until vegetables are desired texture. Less time = more crunchy.

GRANDMA'S SALAD (p. 20)

An Excellent Wife
Weekend Wrap-Up

Using what you learned this week and the verses listed beside each statement, fill in the blanks to reveal truth regarding the excellence of God and the excellence to which we are called.

Hospitality 101: Understanding God's Excellence

- God calls to us through his divine _____ and _____ (2 Peter 1:3).

- God declares us _____ through our faith in Jesus Christ (Romans 5:1).

- God's Word (precepts) is _____ (Psalm 111:7).

- According to the riches of God's glory, He _____ with power (Ephesians 4:16).

- God is always faithful in _____ and _____ (Psalm 145:13).

Hospitality 102: Your Way to Excellence

- The creation of mankind is _____ _____ in the eyes of God (Genesis 1:31).

- We are far more _____ than jewels (Proverbs 31:10).

- _____ in the Lord with _____ your heart (Proverbs 3:5).

- Through His power we bear much _____ (John 15:5).

- Take every _____ captive to obey _____ (2 Corinthians 10:5).

My thoughts concerning this week's study:

_____

_____

_____

_____

_____

_____

_____

_____

_____

_____

_____

_____

_____

_____

_____

_____

_____

_____

_____

_____

_____

_____

_____

Weekend Wrap-Up Desserts

CRÈME BRÛLÉE

The first time I ever had crème brûlée, Todd (my husband) and I had gone to a Brazilian steak house for our anniversary. The waiter was exceptionally friendly and asked if we were celebrating anything special. Of course we were! After our meal, a beautifully adorned, sugar-crusted custard magically appeared as a complimentary dessert. I fell in love with it immediately. Even though we had overeaten, this dessert was wonderfully light and refreshing. It was a year or so later when I received my very own kitchen torch. Now I make crème brûlée for special occasions celebrated at home. Enjoy!

½ c. heavy cream
1 whole egg
½ c. milk
⅛ c. sugar
¼ vanilla bean (split)
Brown sugar
1 egg yolk
Cut-up fruit or berries (optional)

Combine heavy cream, milk, and vanilla bean in small saucepan. Bring to a boil. Remove from heat and steep for 10 minutes with vanilla bean. Scrape bean seeds into the milk mixture and discard hull. With a mixer, combine eggs and sugar. Slowly add milk mixture in a steady stream to eggs and sugar. Strain mixture through a fine strainer and skim any foam. Divide mixture into 4 ramekins (about 4 ounces) set into large baking dish. Pour hot water into baking dish to halfway up the sides of ramekins. Bake at 325° for 25–30 minutes until set (trembles slightly).

Serve warm: Cool 10 minutes. Top with brown sugar, and caramelize sugar with a kitchen torch.

Serve chilled: Cool for 20 minutes. Place in refrigerator for at least 2 hours. Top with brown sugar, and caramelize sugar with a kitchen torch.

Serving Option: Top with berries or fruit if desired.

SHORTBREAD

Shortbread is quite versatile. You can top it with almost anything or eat it by itself. It is also simple and made with ingredients you most likely keep on hand at all times. Be careful not to overbake.

2 sticks butter (softened)
¾ c. sugar
2 ¼ c. flour
Sweetened berries of your choice
Whipped cream (optional)

Cream butter and sugar together. Add flour gradually. Mix well. Press into 9x13-inch casserole dish. Lightly sprinkle with additional sugar. Bake at 350° until golden brown (8–10 minutes). Let cool about 5 minutes before cutting into squares.

Top with sweetened berries and whipped cream.

Mango Salsa, page 72

Working Hands

Are you ready to get your hands dirty? This week we are going to roll up our sleeves and learn about stewardship, attitude, and our contributions to our families. I pray that you will be blessed, encouraged, and motivated to serve your family, your church, and your community. Just remember, love is our motivation. God is love.

> Anyone who does not love does not know God, because God is love.
> (1 John 4:8)

We are called to relationship with our Lord above all else. Out of love for Him, we serve Him. Out of love for Him, He loves in us and through us. Out of love for Him, we serve others. Our service is not to be viewed as a chore or completed like a checklist. Our service is to be an outpouring of love using the unique gifts, talents, skills, and circumstances God has provided. This is our calling:

> Greater love has no one than this, that someone lay down his life for
> his friends. (John 15:13)

As women who fear the Lord, laying down our preferences may be commonplace. We cook family favorites; we take care of household needs; we play nurse, chauffer, chef, teacher, and more, all of which come before your own needs. For many of us, this is only our first job. We also work outside the home to help support the needs of our families, which can soon become exhausting. When we get home in the evenings, the last thing we want to do is figure out what's for dinner and then prepare it. So for this week, your recipes are to help you get in and out of the kitchen quickly when you're in a hurry. Along with the spaghetti from week one, these are my go-to meals.

Remember, living the life we are called to and serving as we should is exhausting, yet fulfilling and rewarding. That is what makes our abundant life priceless.

O Father, help us to love well. Teach us to steward well. Show us how to live well. Give us the grace we need to extend grace to others and the boldness to forgive as we are forgiven. Help me be reflective and honest this week as I study and learn Your Word.

Amen.

Our service is
to be an outpouring of love
using the unique gifts, talents, skills,
and circumstances God has provided.
This is our calling.

Her Hands

She seeks wool and flax, and works with willing hands.

Proverbs 31:13

SHE SEEKS WOOL AND FLAX . . .

Guess what, ladies? This virtuous woman is a shopper! She seeks and selects her wares for her family and for business. We shop and purchase in much the same way. The virtue that separates godliness from greediness is stewardship. Do we seek the best for our families? Do we steward well the multitude of blessings the Lord provides?

Since the very beginning, God has provided for mankind through His creation. Genesis 3:21 says:

> And the LORD God made for Adam and for his wife garments of
> skins and clothed them.

I am thankful that we have advanced beyond the days of tending the fields and pastures in order to clothe ourselves, as today's verse suggests. My appreciation goes out to those who tend the sheep and care for the animals and fields that provide our wool and flax. Though most of us do not find our careers in these areas, we are called to take care and shop wisely. Whether we make our own clothing or choose to purchase them pre-made, pre-washed, and pre-shrunk (with no ironing necessary), we are called to stewardship. We are to shop, steward, and work with willing hands—hands that take delight and pleasure in caring for and handling that which God has provided.

> Do all things without grumbling or disputing, that you may be
> blameless and innocent, children of God without blemish in the
> midst of a crooked and twisted generation, among whom you shine
> as lights in the world, holding fast to the word of life, so that in the
> day of Christ I may be proud that I did not run in vain or labor in
> vain. (Philippians 2:14–16)

Reflection and Application

1. Ephesians 2:10: "For we are his workmanship, created in Christ Jesus for good works, which God prepared beforehand, that we should walk in them." You were created in Christ with a unique purpose. On a scale of 1–10, how willing are your hands to live out this good work? Why is this your answer?

2. Look at your checkbook or budget from last month. How wise are you in your spending? If this is an area where you need help, ask God to give you wisdom for the days and weeks to come. He is always faithful.

3. Do you have the tendency to grumble and complain about your daily tasks? Your finances? Your provisions? What can you do about this so that you find joy in the abundant life God promises to you as His daughter?

4. Look at the passage from Philippians 2:14–16 in our devotion. Highlight or circle all the benefits of not grumbling or complaining.

5. What have you taught your children regarding wise spending and stewardship? Take time this week to explain its importance to them. Write a rough outline of the points you need to make.

6. Look up 1 Peter 4:9, Philippians 2:14, Colossians 3:17, and 1 John 3:18 and write the one that is most relevant to your circumstance. Put it in a prominent place for a reminder.

Prayer / Journal

Reread your answers to the reflection questions. How wise is your spending? Do you grumble and complain? Do you take pleasure in performing your daily tasks? Now pray and ask God to help you as you work with willing hands in such a way that your work is never in vain (Philippians 2:14–16).

_____

_____

_____

_____

_____

_____

_____

_____

_____

_____

_____

_____

_____

_____

_____

_____

_____

_____

Today's Meal
White Sloppy Joes

1 lb. ground meat
½ sm. onion (chopped)
Salt and pepper to taste
Tony's Seasoning
1 can cream of mushroom soup
½ c. sour cream (optional)

Brown ground meat with spices. As meat begins to brown, add onion and cook until meat is done. Drain well and return to skillet. Over medium heat add soup and sour cream (if desired). Stir until bubbly.

Serve over toasted hamburger buns.

Optional Additions:

Put mayo, ketchup, and mustard on buns before topping with meat mixture

Jalapenos (sweet ones are great)

Great with sweet-potato fries, regular fries, or chips of your choice.

This is a quick and easy go-to meal for any night of the week or Sunday afternoons, after church, when all you want is a nap!

Her Provision

She is like the ships of the merchant; she brings her food from afar.

Proverbs 31:14

IN THIS SIMILE, THE MERCHANT SHIPS TO WHICH OUR VIRTUOUS WOMEN ARE COMPARED brought food and goods from other lands to sell and trade. They would return to their homelands with food and supplies that met the needs of their people. By comparison, this business-savvy woman did the same in order to meet the needs of her family and to provide variety in their diets and routines. We learn later, in verse 22, that she made clothing and linen. She used some of these items to clothe her family. Others she took to market to sell and trade for food and household provisions. Her willing hands made sure that the needs of her family were met. This was her unique calling.

In Ephesians 4:1 Paul exhorts us to follow God's call upon our lives.

"I therefore, a prisoner for the Lord, urge you to walk in a manner
worthy of the calling to which you have been called."

To what have you been called? We are all called to provide for the needs of our own families. Whether we work outside the home or not, typically we do the shopping, nursing, cooking, cleaning, and more. With a heavenly perspective on all of this, His provisions and our responsibilities become unique gifts from God to our families. Does this mean that we are to prepare exotic meals from other countries or put the family on a clean-eating diet? Not necessarily. But it does suggest that we do not take the easy way out and order fast food, microwave fish sticks, or keep a good stock of cereal for dinner on a regular basis. We need to be mindful and educated on healthy eating habits and teach them to our children. We should stock our pantries with food that nourishes our bodies. So let's try to mix it up a bit and serve something new. Someone once said, "Variety is the spice of life." Try something new this week. It will bless both you and your family.

Reflection and Application

1. What unique skills did God give you to bless and provide for your family?

2. Write down the meals that you served to your family last week. Was there variety? When was the last time they had those same meals?

3. Not only is physical nourishment important, but we must spiritually feed our souls and the souls of those closest to us. In what ways do you nourish the souls of your family?

4. Ask each member of your family for a meal suggestion. Take out your calendar and make plans to serve it within the next two weeks.

5. Take out a blank calendar or make one for the next two weeks. On that calendar, plan your meals (at least your evening meals). You might need to take inventory of your pantry and freezer before you begin to see what you already have. Be sure to add your family's suggestions from number 4.

6. Read Ephesians 4:1–3. How are you walking in your calling? Which aspect seems to trouble you the most? Humility? Gentleness? Patience? Love? Unity? List steps you can take this week in living this passage.

Prayer/Journal

Take time to thank God for your calling. Ask Him to search your heart and see if there is anything within you that grieves Him (Psalm 139:23–24). He will lead you in the way everlasting.

_____

_____

_____

_____

_____

_____

_____

_____

_____

_____

_____

_____

_____

_____

_____

_____

_____

_____

_____

Today's Meal
2-2-7 Chicken, Ranch-Style Beans, Broccoli Cauliflower Salad

2-2-7 CHICKEN

4 chicken breasts (pounded thin)
Spices: (choose among the following)
Salt and pepper
Tony's Seasoning
Garlic salt, parmesan cheese,
  and Italian breadcrumbs
Cavender's Greek Seasoning
3 T. extra virgin olive oil
BBQ Sauce (optional)

Preheat oven to 350°. Heat oil in a large skillet (high heat). Coat chicken with desired spices. Place chicken breast in hot skillet. Cook for 2 minutes on each side. If skillet is ovenproof, place in hot oven for 7 minutes. If not, transfer chicken to a casserole dish and place in oven for 7 minutes. If BBQ is for you, add sauce and return to oven for 2–3 minutes.

My favorite is garlic parmesan and breadcrumbs. I slice it up and eat it with Caesar salad. You could also add your chicken to the broccoli cauliflower salad.

BROCCOLI CAULIFLOWER SALAD

1 sm. head broccoli
1 sm. head cauliflower
4–6 strips of bacon (fried and crumbled)
½–¾ c. shredded cheddar cheese
1 c. real mayonnaise
2 T. soy sauce
2 T. lemon juice or red wine vinegar
2 t. garlic powder
2–3 T. milk
1 T. sugar

Chop veggies and toss them in a large bowl. Add bacon and cheese. In a small bowl combine mayo, soy sauce, lemon juice (or red wine vinegar), and garlic powder. Stir well. Add enough milk to thin. Sauce should be pourable. Drizzle over salad to coat. Stir well and chill for 30–45 minutes.

This is not necessarily a quick recipe. I suggest making it first and letting it chill while making the remainder of the meal.

Ranch-Style Beans come in a can from any grocery store. Heat well. I like them best with white bread or rolls.

Early to Rise

She rises while it is yet night and provides food
for her household and portions for her maidens.

Proverbs 31:15

YOU CAN LOOK UP SCRIPTURES, QUOTES, AND FAMOUS PEOPLE. MOST ALL OF THEM WILL SAY there is great benefit to getting up early in the morning and starting your day well. Breakfast is important, exercise is healthy, quiet time with God is most beneficial. Starting well takes discipline.

Sprinters and swimmers will tell you that in a race, if you do not get a good start, you lose the race. We live a race every day. The way in which we start matters. The way we begin our day sets the course for the rest.

When my children were young, we listened to Christian radio on the way to school. One afternoon one of my girls mentioned that when we listened to the radio on the way to school, her whole day would go well. But if something went wrong, she would just sing one of the songs she had heard that morning and her day would get better.

A good start for your day may look a bit different. Christian music in the background as your family gets ready for school or work is one way to make a positive difference in your day. Another way to start off on the right foot could be to write out a Scripture and put it in a prominent place for your family to see each day. Again, this will take discipline in the beginning.

God gives us an example in Exodus: When the children of Israel were journeying to the Promised Land, God provided manna. It was only available early in the morning. If they waited too late, the sun melted it away.

Morning by morning they gathered it, each as much as he could eat;
but when the sun grew hot, it melted (Exodus 16:21)

We must not let our opportunity to be fed by God melt away by the busyness of our daily schedules. Try and incorporate prayer, Bible reading, and/or Christian music into your morning routine. Rise early and be fed.

Reflection and Application

1. What types of disciplines do you have that help keep you on track spiritually? What do you do to support the needs of your family's spiritual wellbeing?

2. Think about your morning routine over the past two weeks. How smooth have your days been? Is it a result of your morning rituals? What needs to change?

3. Find a radio or use your phone and play Christian music tomorrow morning while your family gets ready for the day (during breakfast or just in the background). Do this for a week and record your observations.

4. Set your alarm for 20 minutes earlier tomorrow morning. Go to bed 30 minutes earlier tonight. See what God has in store for you.

5. Read Lamentations 3:22–26 What is new every morning? Have you found it to be true for you? Why or why not?

Prayer / Journal

It takes discipline to spend time with the Lord. It is not natural to want to spend time with Him, nor is it easy to get up early in the morning to do so. Pray and ask God to give you the hunger and motivation to make it a part of your day. If not early in the morning, make it priority sometime during the day.

_____

_____

_____

_____

_____

_____

_____

_____

_____

_____

_____

_____

_____

_____

_____

_____

_____

_____

_____

Today's Meal
Pan-Seared Tilapia, Mango Salsa, Rice Pilaf, Roasted Broccoli

PAN-SEARED TILAPIA

6–8 Tilapia filets
Hot sauce
Tony's Seasoning
Cavender's Greek Seasoning
6–8 T. Zatarain's Southern Crispy Fish Fry
3–4 T. butter

Melt 2 tablespoons of butter in a large skillet over medium-high heat. Sprinkle desired amount of spices on fish with a couple drops of hot sauce. Finely dust one side of fish with dry fish fry. Place four filets in skillet, fish-fry side down. Dust other side of fish. Cook about 4 minutes on each side or until completely opaque. Set aside and repeat with remaining filets.

Top with mango salsa if desired.

MANGO SALSA

1 lg. mango or 1 sm. pkg. of frozen, chopped
½ red bell pepper, chopped
2 T. red onion, minced
1 T. fresh cilantro, chopped
1 sm. jalapeno, chopped
2 T. lime juice
Salt and pepper to taste

Mix all ingredients and let chill for 30 minutes.

If you use frozen mango, chop and drain on paper towel before mixing with other ingredients.

RICE PILAF

1 envelope instant brown or wild rice
1 sm. can mushroom pieces, chopped
¼ sm. onion, chopped
1 sm. can water chestnuts, chopped
1 T. extra virgin olive oil
1–2 T. soy sauce (or teriyaki)

Follow microwave directions for rice (open to vent and cook 90 sec). In a small skillet sauté mushrooms, onions and chestnuts. Add rice and stir together. Add sauce and stir until hot throughout.

ROASTED BROCCOLI

1 head broccoli
Extra virgin olive oil
Roasted Garlic and Herb (Weber is good)

Preheat oven to 400°. Chop broccoli in large pieces. Toss in a large bowl with olive oil to coat. Sprinkle seasoning liberally. Pour onto cookie sheets (single layer). Roast for 20–25 minutes until tender.

She Provides

She rises while it is yet night and provides food
for her household and portions for her maidens.

Proverbs 31:15

YESTERDAY WE LOOKED AT HOW TO START STRONG. TODAY WE TAKE A LOOK AT PROVISION, teaching us that we are to provide for our households as well as for those who serve us. We have spent much time this week learning about how to provide for our homes, both physically and spiritually. This verse is no different. Today I want the last four words to jump out at you as they did for me.

She provides . . . **portions for her maidens**.

Why does she do this? She could have easily had her maidens get up and make breakfast for her and her family. However, this is not the case. This woman of God rises early and sees to her family, considering her servants as a part, not separate or undeserving. This is rare, selfless discipline! With the help and teaching of the Holy Spirit, she serves. This is a picture of Christ's servant leadership. Just as Jesus knelt before His disciples and washed their feet, she serves others as an example to her maidens and her family. Does your family serve one another in this way? Do they serve others in your church or community in such a way that honors God? In this day of selfish ambition, selfless service is hard to find. Even more than this is sincere appreciation to those who serve. How do you show appreciation to those who meet your needs?

> In this day of selfish ambition, selfless service is hard to find.

As each has received a gift, use it to serve one another, as good stewards of God's varied grace. (1 Peter 4:10)

Reflection and Application

1. Make a quick list of your morning tasks that help prepare your family for their day. Notice your own selfless acts of service.

2. List the tasks that your family does to help serve others in your home.

3. Look at your lists above. Which is shorter? List ways to involve your family in serving one another.

4. Use your notes from the questions above to discuss with your family ways in which you can serve one another and make everyone's day brighter.

5. Write 1 Peter 4:10 on a piece of paper and put it somewhere in your home where everyone will see it this week.

6. Read Galatians 5:13–26. Describe those who walk according to the flesh.

Prayer / Journal

Write your prayer below and then pray with your family. Ask God to show you how to serve one another in your family, your church, and your community.

_____

_____

_____

_____

_____

_____

_____

_____

_____

_____

_____

_____

_____

_____

_____

_____

_____

_____

Today's Meal
Homemade Pancakes

This is a family favorite. We all love breakfast for supper.

1 c. flour
1 c. milk
2 t. baking powder
2 T. melted butter
1 T. sugar
1 egg (beaten)
½ t. salt

Mix flour, baking powder, salt, and sugar. Stir in melted butter and milk. Add beaten egg and mix. Pour ¼ cup scoops onto hot griddle. Flip when batter is bubbly on top. Cook on second side until brown.

Note: My family loves for me to cook the bacon on the griddle first and then lightly oil the griddle with the bacon grease before I pour the batter. Hey, I am just being honest! At least we do not butter them before adding syrup. I know it is unhealthy, but most really yummy things are!

The Race Begins

> She considers a field and buys it;
> with the fruit of her hand she plants a vineyard.
>
> Proverbs 31:16

WE WERE REMINDED EARLIER THIS WEEK THAT IT IS IMPORTANT TO GET UP EARLY AND SPEND time in prayer and God's Word. Today we learn a little more about why the Proverbs 31 woman must start early. She has a jam-packed day! Can you relate?

She gets up early and cooks breakfast for her family and servants. Then she cleans that up. She gets ready for her day so she can meet her real estate agent, who will show her a piece of property. She buys it and then plants a garden with seeds she's collected and prepared for planting. Whew! The day is not over and I'm already tired.

This woman is not idle, lazy, or bored. I would bet that if this gal would have had a smartphone, she would have spent little or no time on games or social media. She has no time for such things. She works for her family and provides well for them. Compare her work to that of the ant in Proverb 6:6–11. What similarities do you see?

> Go to the ant, O sluggard; consider her ways, and be wise. Without having any chief, officer, or ruler, she prepares her bread in summer and gathers her food in harvest. How long will you lie there, O sluggard? When will you arise from your sleep? A little sleep, a little slumber, a little folding of the hands to rest, and poverty will come upon you like a robber and want like an armed man.

This is a stern warning regarding the stewardship of our time. Let's face it, we take time for that which is important to us—our passions. God uniquely wired us with passion for our families, our jobs/careers, and our hobbies. However, most days we take care of our families as best we can and call it a day. This is not the abundant life to which we are called. We are called to more than survival and going through the motions. We are to abide in Christ (John 15), work with willing hands (Proverbs 31), and do all things without grumbling or complaining (Philippians 2), as unto the Lord (Colossians 3).

Reflection and Application

1. After this much study on Proverbs 31 and reading Proverbs 6 today, how do you compare? Are you more like the ant or the sluggard? What can you do about this?

2. That last paragraph is a tall order. What are your initial feelings regarding your role as a woman who cares for your home and family?

3. Imagine that your day yesterday was filmed from start to finish and you are sitting with a bucket of popcorn and a soda watching it today. How wisely did you use your time? Make a list below of when you might have spent your time more productively.

4. In your own words, describe what you think Jesus meant in John 10:10 when He said He came to give abundant life (life to the full).

5. Using the exercise from number 3 above, make a plan for tomorrow that uses your time more effectively and efficiently. This could be as simple as setting an alarm to get up earlier or going to bed earlier if your day was productive and abundant.

6. Read John 15:1–17. Write down your new ways that you abide in Him.

Prayer/Journal

Ask God to give you the energy, heart, passion, and willingness to work hard for Him and your family. Ask Him to show you how to live the abundant life that He came to give you!

_____

_____

_____

_____

_____

_____

_____

_____

_____

_____

_____

_____

_____

_____

_____

_____

_____

_____

Today's Meal
Minestrone Goulash

2 lbs. ground beef, browned
1 med. onion, chopped
1 can whole kernel corn, drained
1 c. minute rice
1 can diced tomatoes with chilis
1 can ranch-style beans
Shredded or sliced cheese (optional)
2 cans minestrone soup

In a large soup pot, brown meat and season to taste. Add onion and simmer until onions are clear. Add tomatoes, beans, soup, and corn to the pot. Bring to a boil. Add rice. Simmer 30 minutes. Enjoy with crackers on the side.

Note: I prefer to use 1 cup of frozen corn kernels instead of the can if I have it.

Serving Suggestion: We like to serve it with a sprinkle or slice of cheese on top of individual bowls.

Working Hands
Weekend Wrap-Up

Using what you learned this week and the verses listed beside each statement, fill in the blanks to remind you of God's work in you as well as the work to which you have been called.

Hospitality 101: Understanding God's Work

- God's work began at _____ and it is for us (Genesis 1:29–30).

- You are God's _____ created for good works (Ephesians 2:10).

- God provides what you need _____ by _____ (Exodus 16:21–22).

- God's Spirit _____ and _____ us of all Jesus said (John 14:26).

- God _____ our steps (Proverbs 16:9).

Hospitality 102: Our Willing Hands

- We are to work without _____ or _____ (Philippians 2:14).

- We must _____ _____ of our calling (Ephesians 4:1).

- Our job is to gather what we and our families _____ each day (Exodus 16:16).

- We should _____ one another as good _____ of God's grace (1 Peter 4:10).

- If we _____ God in all things, He makes our paths _____ (Proverbs 3:6).

My thoughts concerning this week's study:

_____

_____

_____

_____

_____

_____

_____

_____

_____

_____

_____

_____

_____

_____

_____

_____

_____

_____

_____

_____

_____

Weekend Wrap-Up Desserts

DUMP CAKE

1 can crushed pineapple
1 can favorite pie filling
  (we like strawberry or blackberry best)
1 box yellow or white cake mix
1 stick butter (melted)
1 c. chopped pecans (optional)

In a 9x13-inch baking dish, pour pineapple and pie filling and stir well. Sprinkle dry cake mix all over the top. Pour butter on top and sprinkle with pecans. Bake at 350° for 30–35 minutes.

Serve warm with vanilla ice cream.

STRAWBERRY SURPRISE

2 c. sliced strawberries
½ c. sugar
1 Pillsbury pie crust
3–4 T. butter (softened)
½ c. sugar
1 T. cinnamon
Cool Whip or favorite whipped topping

Combine strawberries and ½ cup sugar; let chill. Flatten pie crust on cookie sheet or circular pizza pan. Spread butter on pie crust. Combine ½ cup sugar and cinnamon, and sprinkle on buttered pie crust. Bake at 350° for 15–20 minutes or until crust is golden brown on bottom. Immediately use a pizza cutter or butter knife to cut pie crust into strips and allow to cool.

To Serve: Pour ¼ cup of strawberries in a bowl and top with Cool Whip. Place 3–4 broken pie strips on the side. Enjoy!

P.S. The surprise is how easy and delicious this is.

BBQ Meatballs, page 102

Her Character

As we examine the characteristics of the ideal woman in this poem, we will find that it is all about perspective. When we seek first the kingdom of God and His righteousness, we gain a heavenly perspective and begin to see ourselves as strong in the strength of the Lord and resourceful and content when we rely on His provision.

Do you notice the freedom in that? Too many times we feel like it is all up to us to take care of the world around us. But look again at the words from the paragraph above: kingdom of God, His righteousness, heavenly perspective, strength of the Lord, His provision. Girl, this is good stuff! This is what makes us priceless. It's God with us, in us, and through us. So take a deep breath and relax. Let your worries, cares, and stresses fall away. It is not up to you. You cannot do it all, and you do not have to.

> But Jesus looked at them and said, "With man this is impossible,
> but with God all things are possible." (Matthew 19:26)

With the help of the Holy Spirit, we can do all things. We can live out our unique giftings and serve with gladness. The godly character given to us as a rare and unique gift is what gives us meaning and purpose. It is what makes us priceless in the sight of God and man. This gift was given to you but is meant to benefit others, no matter the task at hand.

When your task is to feed a crowd, use this week's menus. They are meant to be a blessing to larger groups around the table. They can be prepared for your family, for hospitality nights with friends, or shared at a potluck dinner. You can also provide these meals to friends and their families in a time of need or celebration.

Heavenly Daddy, instill in me the fruit of the Spirit. Nourish it and help it to grow in abundance. Help me to be full of joy, hope, peace, and love. Teach me to be patient, kind, good, and gentle, and guide my steps as I walk in steadfast faithfulness. Thank you for your Spirit that helps me daily.

Amen.

Jesus alone gives rest for your soul.
He alone can take your load
and carry it for you.
Only Jesus gives you
the strength you need to face the
challenges of your life.
Trust Him!

She Is Strong

She dresses herself with strength and makes her arms strong.

Proverbs 31:17

HOW CAN YOU TELL IF A WOMAN IS STRONG? PHYSICALLY, IT'S HER ABILITY TO LIFT, CARRY, pull, push, and work for long periods of time. We know she is strong when we see her handle a heavy load. Spiritually, it's her ability to stand firm in her convictions, to fight against the schemes of the devil, to lift others up with words and actions that encourage them to keep going. We know she is strong when we see her rely on the Lord to handle her heavy load.

This strong parallel reminds me of Ephesians 6:10 when Paul tells us to be strong in the Lord and in the strength of His might. In verse 16 he tells us that in all circumstances we are to take up the shield of faith, with which we can extinguish all the flaming darts of the evil one. These verses, along with Proverbs 31:17, remind us that it takes both physical and spiritual strength to be the virtuous women we are called to be.

So why do we feel so weak at times? What are we to do when we feel like our strength and hope are gone? Jesus answers these questions in Matthew 11:28–30:

> "Come to me, all who labor and are heavy laden, and I will give you
> rest. Take my yoke upon you, and learn from me, for I am gentle
> and lowly in heart, and you will find rest for your souls. For my
> yoke is easy, and my burden is light."

I pray you really grasp this. Jesus alone gives rest for your soul. He alone can take your load and carry it for you. Only Jesus gives you the strength you need to face the challenges of your life. Trust Him! Bring your burdens to the Lord, learn from Him, put on the armor of God, and be clothed in strength. As you practice walking in this way, your arms become strong—strong enough to carry the shield of faith and to encourage others, strong enough to wield the sword of the Spirit with confidence, strong enough to let go and give your burden to the Lord and then run freely the race set before you.

Reflection and Application

1. How well do you relate to the passage and message today? From where does your strength come?

2. In what areas of your life do you feel the weakest? What can you do about it?

3. What do you typically do when you feel weak? Is this beneficial or harmful?

4. Nehemiah 8:10 reminds us that the joy of the Lord is our strength. Write the name of a song or the lyrics that bring joy to your heart and strength to your spirit.

5. Share with at least one other person the song and lyrics you wrote above. Tell them how good God is and how He gives you strength.

6. Read 2 Corinthians 12:9–10. List the ways in which you relate to Paul in this passage.

Prayer / Journal

Confess your weaknesses to the Lord in prayer. Ask Him to show you how to wear the armor of God. Let Him strengthen your arms. If you are feeling strong today, ask God to show you someone who needs encouragement, and stand strong with them.

_____

_____

_____

_____

_____

_____

_____

_____

_____

_____

_____

_____

_____

_____

_____

_____

_____

_____

_____

_____

Today's Meal
Shrimp Chowder

12–16 oz. whole kernel corn
½ lb. Velveeta (¼ large box)
1 can cream-style corn
1 lb. small uncooked shrimp (peeled)
1 can cream of celery soup
2 T. liquid shrimp boil
1 pt. half and half
Red pepper flakes
½ c. butter
Butter-flavored potato flakes

In a 2-quart pot, combine butter, soup, and corn. Over medium heat melt butter and simmer as you add cubed Velveeta. When mixture begins to thicken, add half and half. Meanwhile, fill a small saucepan ¾ full of water, add liquid shrimp boil. Bring to a boil and add shrimp. When shrimp comes to a boil, allow to boil 3 minutes and remove from heat. Let stand for five minutes and strain (saving liquid). Add shrimp to chowder. Simmer on low for 10 minutes. Add pepper flakes and/or liquid from shrimp boil to taste. Thicken with potato flakes to desired consistency by adding ⅛ cup at a time.

This is great fare for a winter evening. It is best served with club crackers. You can also garnish your serving with freshly chopped green onions and parsley.

She Is Content

> She perceives that her merchandise is profitable.
> Her lamp does not go out at night.
>
> Proverbs 31:18

SHE PERCEIVES PROFIT. HOW MANY TIMES DO WE CATCH OUR HEARTS FULL OF DISCONTENT-ment after a long day of work? We always seem to want a little more for all of our effort. We see what others have and wish we could have the same or a little more. Sure, it is fun to dream. But it is not okay to be dissatisfied or discontent with what you have. We should never allow what we do or do not possess to determine our level or capacity for joy.

As we look at the character of the Proverbs 31 woman, we see that she is content with what she has and is proud of and thankful for God's provision. Last week we saw all of her hard work. When we work hard and have food, clothing, healthy families, and shelter, we can be proud and take joy in our accomplishments, being thankful to God for the skills and abilities that help make those things happen. But be careful! All of the honor and glory go to Him and not ourselves. We cannot become proud at this time. We must humbly reflect and perceive rightly that all we have comes from our heavenly Daddy. He makes it possible for us to work. He alone provides for our needs. He deserves the praise.

If you struggle with discontentment, you are not alone. Be thankful to God for all He has done. Count your blessings. You cannot be discontent and thankful at the same time. Let all God has done for you resonate in your heart in a way that any discontentment dissolves in light of God's goodness and glory.

Although discontentment mostly has a negative connotation, there is a place for holy discontentment. We are strangers, aliens in this world. God has placed eternity in our hearts (Ecclesiastes 3:11). This world is not our home. However, while here we are to bring Him glory.

2 Corinthians 5:9: So whether we are at home or away, we make it our aim to please him.

Reflection and Application

1. Reflect on your current level of contentment. If you had to place a number value (scale 1 to 10), how content are you with your finances, marriage, home, work? Is there anything within your power to change any of these circumstances? If so, list below what you can do to improve.

2. What does it mean to you that God has placed eternity in your heart?

3. Is there anything in your life for which you have sought and/or received credit that belongs to God? If so, what is it and how can you give God the glory?

4. Always wanting more leads to discontentment and covetousness. List the top five blessings in your life.

5. Name one person with whom you can share your top five list. Share this week.

6. Read Daniel 4:28–37. In your own words, explain the danger of pride and taking credit for the prosperity in your life.

Prayer / Journal

Thank God for the blessings in your life. Confess discontentment and pray that God will show you His perspective on your circumstances.

_____

_____

_____

_____

_____

_____

_____

_____

_____

_____

_____

_____

_____

_____

_____

_____

_____

_____

_____

_____

_____

_____

Today's Meal
Chicken Enchiladas, Beans and Rice

SOUR CREAM CHICKEN ENCHILADAS

1 chicken, boiled and deboned
4 t. olive oil
1 can green chilies (optional)
1 can cream of chicken soup
12 flour tortillas
10 oz. Monterey jack cheese
1 med. onion (chopped)
1 c. sour cream
1 t. cumin
Picante sauce

Sauté onion in oil. Add chicken and just enough broth to make chicken moist. Add salt and cumin. Heat well. Make sauce with soup, sour cream, and 2–4 tablespoons of picante sauce. Heat until hot. Put a small amount of chicken mixture in each tortilla and roll into enchilada. Place all enchiladas in a greased 9x13-inch baking dish. Pour sauce over the enchiladas. Sprinkle with grated cheese and bake for 30 min. at 350°. Garnish with green chilies and picante sauce.

REFRIED BEANS

1 T. butter
1 can refried beans
2 T. onion (finely chopped)
Garlic salt
Taco Bell's Mild Sauce

In a small saucepan, melt butter and sauté onion. Add beans and 2 tablespoons water. Stir until smooth. Add garlic salt and sauce to taste.

MEXICAN-STYLE RICE

2 T. extra virgin olive oil
1 ½ c. long grain rice
1 cube chicken bouillon
¼ c. favorite salsa
1 ¾ c. boiling water

In a medium saucepan, sauté rice in oil until light brown. Dissolve bouillon cube in water. Pour broth and salsa into rice. Bring to a boil. Reduce heat to medium-low and cook until water is absorbed (12–15 minutes). Flake with a fork.

She Is Perceptive

She perceives that her merchandise is profitable.
Her lamp does not go out at night.

Proverbs 31:18

I KNOW THIS VERSE LOOKS FAMILIAR, BUT YOU HAD TO KNOW THAT WE WOULD NOT SKIP THE second half of it. For several days/weeks now we have heard how busy this woman is. Today we see her reflect on her day and take note that her work was successful, beneficial, and profitable. Can you look back and see that you honored God in all that you accomplished today? If so, your work (even if incomplete) was successful, beneficial, and profitable.

We also see in this verse that the lamp does not go out at night. What does she do into the night? My guess is that she does the same things we do. She gets the children to bed, cleans up the day's mess in the house, and prepares for tomorrow. She reflects on her day and prepares for the next. I wonder, as I read this proverb, what must she be thinking? I know I am exhausted just reading about her daily ventures.

Then it hit me: it is all a matter of perspective. When you reflect upon your day, be careful not to fall into the all-too-familiar trap of making yourself out to be a martyr for all your hard work. The danger lies not in our busyness but in the distractibility of our chaos.

In Luke 10:38–42 we read about Martha. She is often blamed for working too hard and not taking time to sit with Jesus, as Mary did. But look again around the fourth word of verse 40. Martha was what? Distracted! Distracted from what? From being filled with the fullness of joy while she had Jesus, her Lord, in her home. The danger in much serving and all of our busyness is that we lose perspective. We find ourselves distracted from the joy of having a family when our perspective turns to self. We get distracted when our perspective shifts to **our** preferences and expectations instead of delighting in fulfilling our calling as wives, mothers, sisters, daughters, friends, and employees. I pray that God gives us His perspective on our repetitious chaos and helps us see the awesome responsibility we have to serve others as a blessing.

> The danger in much serving and all of our busyness is that we lose perspective.

Reflection and Application

1. As you reflect on your day, list areas of productivity.

2. Do you feel as though your day brought honor to the Lord? Others in your life?

3. How does your perspective on your daily tasks need to change?

4. Read Luke 10:38–42. Make a list of the things you think Martha was busy doing.

5. List the tasks in your day that tend to become distractions from the joy you have in the Lord.

6. Make a to-do list for your tasks that lie ahead tomorrow or later today.

Prayer / Journal

Look at the lists that you made in the last three questions. Pray over your lists. Ask God to give you a fresh perspective on your daily busyness. Ask Him to remove the distractibility and replace it with a sense of fulfillment and joy.

_____

_____

_____

_____

_____

_____

_____

_____

_____

_____

_____

_____

_____

_____

_____

_____

_____

_____

_____

_____

_____

Today's Meal
Chicken Spaghetti, Garlic Bread, Garden Salad

1 chicken, boiled and deboned (save broth)
1 med. package of spaghetti
½ lb. Velveeta
1 can diced tomatoes with chilis
1 can cream of mushroom soup
12 oz. cheddar cheese (shredded)
1 onion
1 bell pepper
2 cloves of garlic

Cook spaghetti and chopped vegetables in broth from chicken. Noodles should absorb almost all the broth.

In a saucepan combine tomatoes, cream of mushroom soup, Velveeta, and 6 oz. shredded cheese. Cook on medium-low just until cheese melts.

When noodles are done, add soup mixture and chicken. Stir together and pour into 9x13-inch pan. Top with remaining shredded cheese and bake at 350° until cheese is melted on top (about 10–15 minutes).

See page 12 for garlic bread and page 24 for garden salad, or choose your favorite recipes to go with your spaghetti.

She Is Resourceful

TAKE A MINUTE TO LOOK AT YOUR HANDS. NOTICE THE LINES AND CREASES ON YOUR PALMS and the backs. Each line, crease, freckle, and mark makes you and your service to God unique. God took great care in creating you and me. He gave us hands to serve, work, give, and worship.

Make a mental list of all that you do with your hands in a day. How many of those things are related to serving? Giving? Helping? Praising? Today's verses show us that work and giving happen with the same hands. Over the last few days we have established that our hands should rarely be idle. We are all busy. However, what purpose does your busyness serve?

Consider this: In Colossians 3:23, we are called to work in this way: "Whatever you do, work heartily, as for the Lord and not for men."

Matthew 25:31–46 explains Jesus's perspective on our service. Verses 35 and 36 say:

> "For I was hungry and you gave me food, I was thirsty and you gave me drink, I was a stranger and you welcomed me, I was naked and you clothed me, I was sick and you visited me, I was in prison and you came to me."

A few verses later Jesus says, "Truly, I say to you, as you did it to one of the least of my brothers, you did it to me."

God gave us two hands with which to honor Him. They are never to be idle but willing and ready to work and serve as He commands, and then to worship and praise as our hearts are gladdened through service to others.

Reflection and Application

1. What have you done "for the least of these"?

2. What do you do with downtime? Is it productive?

3. Write your list of what your hands do in a day. Write an "s" beside tasks that serve, a "w" for worship, and "g" for give. Notice any trends or missing categories.

4. Trace one of your hands on the journal page in the space provided. On it, write one way to serve others, one way to worship, and one way to give that you did not list above.

5. Read Matthew 25:31–46. In your own words and in today's world, what can you do "for the least of these"?

6. Share with a friend how you are going to use your hands this week to work and serve. Ask her to hold you accountable to do it.

Prayer/Journal

Ask God how and who He would have you serve this week and what He would have you give in His name.

_____

_____

_____

_____

_____

_____

_____

_____

_____

_____

_____

_____

_____

_____

_____

_____

_____

_____

_____

_____

_____

_____

_____

_____

Today's Meal
BBQ Meatballs, Cheesy Hash Brown Potato Casserole, Broccoli Cauliflower Salad

BBQ MEATBALLS

Meatballs:
12 oz. evaporated milk
3 lbs. lean ground beef
2 c. oatmeal
2 ½ t. salt
2 ½ t. chili powder
1 t. garlic powder
1 t. pepper
1 c. finely chopped onion
1 egg

Sauce:
2 c. ketchup
2 T. liquid smoke
1 tsp. garlic powder
1 ½ c. brown sugar

Combine meatball ingredients. Form balls (a little larger than a golf ball) and place in two 9x13-inch pans. Mix sauce ingredients and pour over meatballs. Bake at 350° for 45 minutes to an hour.

CHEESY HASH BROWN CASSEROLE

1 can cream of mushroom soup
¾ c. sour cream
1 T. melted butter
1 T. dried onion flakes
Salt and pepper to taste
1 lb. frozen shredded hash brown potatoes
4 oz. shredded cheddar
½ c. cornflakes

Lightly grease the bottom or a 9x9-inch baking dish. In a large bowl mix soup, butter, sour cream, onion flakes, and salt and pepper. Stir in hash browns and half of the cheese. Pour into prepared baking dish and sprinkle with remaining cheese and crushed cornflakes. Bake for 45 minutes at 350°.

Note: This makes a good size for a family. However, it is very easy to double and take to a covered-dish event. Bake in a 9x13-inch pan.

BROCCOLI CAULIFLOWER SALAD (p. 68)

She Is Prepared

She is not afraid of snow for her household, for all her household are clothed in scarlet. She makes bed coverings for herself; her clothing is fine linen and purple.

Proverbs 31:21–22

THE BOY SCOUTS HAVE THE MOTTO: BE PREPARED. I BELIEVE OUR STUDY LEADS US TO THE same necessity. The reason we are not to fear the winter for our household is because we are prepared. We are physically ready for winter. We have clothing, firewood, working heaters, food, etc. that will get us through the cold months of the year. This takes discipline and a good work ethic.

But what about spiritual preparation? Is your family ready for a crisis? Are you prepared for battle with sin and Satan? God promises to never leave us or forsake us. Just as He was with Moses and Joshua, He is with us. Though the discipline and work ethic may differ for our spiritual preparedness, it is just as—and even more—necessary. Hebrews 13:6 says,

> We can confidently say, "The Lord is my helper; I will not fear; what
> can man do to me?"

But what is our part? How are we to prepare for battle and crises? Ephesians 6:10–20 tells us how to effectively utilize the whole armor of God. 2 Timothy 2:15 tells us to study to show ourselves approved by God. James 1:22–25 tells us to be doers of the Word. When we study God's Word and do what it says, we prepare for battle. Then, we will, no doubt, be ready for whatever comes our way.

I have heard it said that if you are not currently going through a trial, just hang on. It is coming. James 1:2–4 reminds us:

> Count it all joy, my brothers, **when** you meet trials of various kinds,
> for you know that the testing of your faith produces steadfastness.
> And let steadfastness have its full effect, that you may be perfect and
> complete, lacking in nothing.

Oh, to come through the winter with our souls perfect, complete, lacking nothing.

Reflection and Application

1. Are you afraid for physical or spiritual winter? How prepared are you for the trials ahead?

2. Look ahead. Do you see potential trials in your future? What might be headed your way?

3. Based on 2 Timothy 2:15, in what ways do you study to show yourself to God as one approved?

4. Read Ephesians 6:10–20. List the parts of the armor of God. Highlight the one piece that you struggle with the most to wear daily.

5. Look in a mirror. Note one thing that needs to change (hair, makeup, teeth brushing). Read James 1:22–25. Based upon God's Word, write down one thing that needs to change.

6. Read Matthew 6:25–34. Record your thoughts.

Prayer / Journal

Based upon your answer to question number 2 and Matthew chapter 6, pray and ask God to remove any tendency you might have to be anxious about tomorrow. Give Him your burden. He can handle it!

_____

_____

_____

_____

_____

_____

_____

_____

_____

_____

_____

_____

_____

_____

_____

_____

_____

_____

_____

Today's Meal
Jambalaya

3 T. canola oil
1 pkg. polska kielbasa sausage
3 cloves garlic
1 lg. onion
2–3 chicken breasts
1 T. Kitchen Bouquet
Tony's Seasoning
2 c. rice

Heat oil in a large dutch oven or 3-quart pot. Add chopped onions and garlic, and sauté. Cut sausage and raw chicken into bite-sized pieces. Add sausage to onion and lightly brown. Add ¼ cup water and chicken. Sprinkle with Tony's. Place a lid on pot and simmer for 30 minutes or until chicken is done. Stir occasionally. Break up the meat and add enough water to cook rice (about 3 ½ cups). Add rice and Kitchen Bouquet. Bring to a boil, stir, reduce heat to medium-low and cover. Do not remove lid until rice is done (about 20 minutes). When rice is fluffy, remove the lid and turn off the heat. Allow rice to absorb any remaining water. Serve the meat mixture over the rice.

Note: Minute rice can be used. Follow directions on the box for water amounts and cooking time.

Her Character
Weekend Wrap-Up

Using what you learned this week and the verses listed beside each statement, fill in the blanks to remind you of God's character and the blessing He is in you and through you to others.

Hospitality 101: Understanding His Character

- He is _____ and _____ (Matthew 11:29).

- He has put _____ in our hearts (Ecclesiastes 3:11).

- God looks at the _____ of man, not his outer _____ (1 Samuel 16:7).

- In His _____ is the _____ and _____ of all mankind (Job 12:10).

- He _____ us with everything _____ to do His _____ (Hebrews 13:21).

Hospitality 102: Her Godly Character

- We are _____ in the power of His _____ (Ephesians 6:10).

- In whatever _____, we are to be _____ (Philippians 4:12).

- We _____ to Jesus the _____ and _____ of our faith (Hebrews 12:2).

- We should to _____ in the _____ of Jesus (Colossians 3:17).

- We _____ ourselves to God as one _____ (2 Timothy 2:15).

My thoughts concerning this week's study:

_____

_____

_____

_____

_____

_____

_____

_____

_____

_____

_____

_____

_____

_____

_____

_____

_____

_____

_____

_____

_____

_____

_____

_____

Weekend Wrap-Up Desserts

DARN-GOOD PIES

I first had this pie at a potluck lunch when I was teaching second grade. My principal brought these pies, and I hounded her for weeks until she shared the recipe.

2 sticks butter (melted)
1 lg. can crushed pineapple
6 eggs (beaten)
2 t. vanilla
3 c. sugar
2 c. coconut
¼ c. flour
2 unbaked 9-inch pie crusts

Combine eggs and butter in a large mixing bowl. slowly whisking. Mix dry ingredients in separate bowl. Slowly add to egg mixture. Add remaining ingredients. Pour mixture into pie crusts, dividing evenly. Bake 10 minutes at 450°. Reduce heat to 350° and bake an additional 30 minutes.

I like it warm and I like it cold. Try it both ways. It is a rich, sweet pie that goes fast. I always make two. Feel free to halve the recipe for your family. However, you can always freeze one for later. Be ready to share the recipe. Your friends will hound you for it too!

HOMEMADE CRUNCHY CARAMEL CANDY BARS

Once again, I got this recipe at a school potluck. Teachers and principals share the best recipes!

90 club crackers
½ c. whole milk
1 c. butter
1 tsp. vanilla
2 c. graham cracker crumbs
1 c. butterscotch chips
1 c. packed brown sugar
1 c. Nutella
⅓ c. sugar

Line 9x13-inch pan with 1 layer of crackers (cut to fit). In a large saucepan melt butter over medium heat. Combine graham cracker crumbs and sugars. Add to melted butter. Stir in milk and vanilla. Bring to a boil and stir for 4–5 minutes. Remove from heat. Pour half of mixture over crackers. Add a layer of crackers, last half of caramel mixture, and finish with crackers. In a microwave bowl, melt butterscotch chips, add Nutella, and stir until smooth. Spread over crackers and chill for 1 hour. Cut into bars and enjoy!

These yummy, crispy caramel bars also go fast. They are a hit at parties. The recipe makes a lot. I usually cut into 1.5-inch squares for larger parties. Other times I cut them about the size of the crackers but make them even.

Taquitos, page 120

Be a Blessing

Counting our blessings is one thing, but this week I hope to inspire you to be a blessing in your home. Then, be a blessing in your community and in your church. It can be a challenge when we look at our responsibility to enrich the lives of our families, put on the armor of God each day, and fill others' hearts with the love of God. I believe we are up for this challenge with the help of the Holy Spirit. Taking quality time to laugh with and love our families is key to relationship. We must stop taking ourselves too seriously and being so hard on ourselves.

As a blessing to your family, I challenge you to schedule time with them. Plan it and guard it like it is as important as a job interview. When our girls were still living at home, some of my best memories were game nights and meals around the table. There are many lessons that were learned when spending time together as a family: healthy competition, winning graciously or losing with a good attitude, taking turns, letting others choose the game and be happy playing even when it isn't your favorite, how to let go and have fun and be silly . . . These qualities are not only valuable in the home but prove to be valuable in the lives of our families as we go into our communities. If you do not yet have this in your home, I would encourage you to start, even if it is only once a month at the beginning. Your time together will create priceless memories and provide priceless life lessons for everyone. In order to empower and enable you to be free to enjoy the company of your family, this week's menu suggestions can be shared during game night and family time. Most can be served on paper plates and eaten with fingers, though you may have to be a little more careful with the Mexican chicken. Enjoy your family this week. Be a blessing and teach them how to bless one another.

Heavenly Daddy, bless our homes this week. Help us to love well and make a priority of spending time together. Strengthen us as a family unit, that we may go out and love our community in a way that leads them to You.

Amen.

*In the bounty of
God's vast provisions,
we possess the capacity for bringing
honor and blessing
to our husbands and families.*

Blessing Her Husband

IN THE MIDST OF A POEM ALL ABOUT HER, WHY DO WE FIND THIS VERSE ALL ABOUT HER HUS-band? I am sure you have heard the saying, "Behind every great man there is a great woman." While this may not always be the case, we've been studying the most precious of women who obviously fears the Lord. How could her husband be anything but well known and respected in the gates, in his home, and everywhere else?

> An excellent wife is the crown of her husband, but she who brings shame is like rottenness in his bones (Proverbs 12:4). We were created to be his helper, not rottenness to his bones.

> Then the LORD God said, "It is not good that the man should be alone; I will make him a helper fit for him." (Genesis 2:18)

As wives, we have the power to influence for both good and bad. Once you are married and become one flesh (Genesis 2:24), your personal reputation becomes the reputation you have as a couple. Just as our husbands' actions and words have an effect on our lives, what we do or fail to do—our choices, our words, our attitudes, our moods—have an effect on our husbands. When we take care to represent God well, we bring Him honor. When we honor God and fear Him in our actions and words, we bring honor to our husbands. Our husbands should be well known and respected wherever they go because of our behavior, not in spite of it.

With the help of the Lord, we have the ability to help others. In the bounty of His vast provisions, we possess the capacity for bringing honor and blessing to our husbands and families.

Reflection and Application

1.   What is your ministry as a couple? Are you both well respected because of your walk with the Lord?

2.   Look back at our devotion for today. According to Proverbs 12:4, are you a crown to your husband's head that he proudly shows off?

3.   How does your marriage bring honor to God? What is your contribution?

4.   Read Job 2:9. What were Job's wife's thoughts about his condition?

5.   How did Job's wife influence Job's faith?

6.   Celebrate your husband this week. Brag on him to your children and others in front of him.

Prayer / Journal

Thank God for your husband today. Ask God to show you how to honor him more or better. Ask God to show you how your marriage can be a ministry to others.

_____

_____

_____

_____

_____

_____

_____

_____

_____

_____

_____

_____

_____

_____

_____

_____

_____

_____

_____

_____

Today's Meal
Mexican Chicken

1 whole chicken (boiled and deboned)
1 T. garlic salt
2 cans cream of chicken soup
1 t. salt
1 sm. onion
1 T. chili powder
1 can fiesta cheese soup
1 bag tortilla chips
10–12 oz. shredded cheddar cheese

Add all ingredients except chips and shredded cheese to a 9x13-inch baking dish. Bake at 375° for 20 minutes. Top with a single layer of chips and cheese. Save some chips for dipping and scooping while you eat. Return dish to the oven long enough to melt cheese.

Serve with taquitos or rolled tacos (Delimex is a good brand).

Blessing Her Community

She makes linen garments and sells them; she delivers sashes to the merchant.

Proverbs 31:24

AMONG SO MANY OTHER THINGS, OUR PROVERBS 31 FRIEND IS A BUSINESSWOMAN. PART OF the reason her husband is so well known and respected is because of her work ethic and resourcefulness. She deals honestly as she sells her goods. She takes care to deliver the best and to never cut corners. Merchants know her and her merchandise well. She brings honor to her husband and her family by the work she does and the wares she sells. The quality of her work is never questioned. Just a few days ago, we noticed that she looked at her merchandise and perceived that it was profitable. Now we see that others understand the same. Can you imagine her attitude of gratitude as she works to help support her family?

When was the last time that your work brought honor to those you love? Do your daily tasks reflect your love for the Lord or are they drudgery and mind-numbing? What is your attitude about your work? Would others be surprised to find out that you are a Christian because of the way you walk, talk, or do business?

> And whatever you do, in word or deed, do everything in the name
> of the Lord Jesus, giving thanks to God the Father through him.
> (Colossians 3:17)

When we go about our daily tasks in the name of the Lord, we too can look at our day's work and perceive it as profitable. When we view our work as a blessing both for ourselves and to others, we are all blessed by the beauty with which we serve: the beauty of God's love in us and through us.

The loving hands of a virtuous woman who works inside her home and in her community only serve to enrich the lives of her family and the lives of those around her. Whose lives do you enrich as you work and serve the Lord?

Reflection and Application

1. The second paragraph for today has a whole list of soul-searching questions. Reread it and then write your thoughts below.

2. Reflect on your daily tasks. Do you view them as busyness or business? What do you think is the difference?

3. Based on your answer to question number 2 above, what needs to change in your perspective and/or schedule?

4. Prepare a list of your family's favorite activities. Make it a point this week to engage in at least two of these activities with a willing heart that seeks to enrich others.

5. After you have completed the task in question number 4, write down your reflections (family responses, feelings, outcomes).

6. List the ways you enrich the lives of people in your community. If your list is short or nonexistent, consider ways that you will serve sometime within the next two weeks.

Prayer/Journal

Thank God today for your daily tasks. Ask Him to show you how to be a blessing as you serve your family and community.

_____

_____

_____

_____

_____

_____

_____

_____

_____

_____

_____

_____

_____

_____

_____

_____

_____

_____

_____

_____

Today's Meal
Homemade Taquitos, Salsa, Green Sauce, Crema

TAQUITOS

½ med. onion
3–5 Roma tomatoes
2 jalapenos
Salt and pepper
2 lb. ground meat
20 fresh flour tortillas

In a medium saucepan, cover whole peppers and tomatoes with water and boil until tomatoes split and peppers change color and soften. In a skillet, brown meat with onion. Drain and set aside. Drain tomato and peppers and place in a blender. Blend until liquified. Pour mixture over meat in skillet. Add salt and pepper to taste. Simmer on low until almost all juice is gone.

Roll 3–4 tablespoons of meat tightly into each tortilla.

Serve with one or all sauces.

CREMA

8 oz. sour cream
4–6 T. milk
Garlic salt to taste

Whisk together and enjoy on taquitos or any Mexican dish.

GREEN SAUCE

2 ripe avocados
4 T. sour cream
Garlic salt to taste
Black pepper to taste
Milk

Mash avocados well. Add sour cream and spices to taste. Add milk to desired consistency.

Serve with taquitos or any Mexican dish.

SALSA

1 can Mexican-style stewed tomatoes
8 oz. salsa verde
1 jalapeno pepper (seeded)
1 serrano pepper
½ bunch of cilantro
2 lg. clove garlic
½ c. chopped green-onion tops
Salt to taste

Combine all ingredients in a blender and serve with chips.

Dressed for Success

> Strength and dignity are her clothing, and she laughs at the time to come.
>
> Proverbs 31:25

GETTING DRESSED SEEMS SO SIMPLE. WE DO IT MOST DAYS WITHOUT EVEN THINKING. SURE, we look at the weather and the events of the day, and then we dress accordingly.

This is exactly what we should do spiritually, only with much thought and strategy. We can look at what we know lies ahead and reach for what we need. If we need gladness of heart, we can reach for Psalm 9 and "give thanks with our whole heart and recount His wonderful deeds." If we need wisdom, we can read passages from the book of Proverbs and ask God to provide wisdom. God "will give wisdom to us generously without reproach" (James 1:5). God's Word contains what we need to face any situation.

Because we never fully know what our day will bring, we cannot know what conflict or crisis may loom in the near future. We must prepare! Ephesians 6:10–20 tells us exactly how to prepare for every occasion. The six pieces of the armor of God should be worn at all times. It is only with His full protection and prayer that we can withstand the enemy and his schemes. Not only that, but we have the power and weaponry to defeat him and put him in his place. As children of God, with the armor of God, we have the authority of God through His Word, the Bible.

The Bible is full of information, training, and help for you as you face the day. It is your teacher, your strength, and your sword!

> All Scripture is breathed out by God and profitable for teaching, for reproof, for correction, and training in righteousness, that the man of God may be complete, equipped for every good work. (2 Timothy 3:16)

This enables us to walk out the door with strength and dignity every day.

Reflection and Application

1. What do you need in order to face your day with strength and dignity?

2. How do you physically prepare for your day?

3. How do you spiritually prepare for your day?

4. List the items that you grab on your way out the door each day. Briefly tell the reason you need each item.

5. List the pieces of the armor of God in Ephesians 6:10–20. Briefly tell the reason why you need each item.

6. Based on your answers to question number 5, write down the piece of armor you need most today and why.

Prayer / Journal

Strength and dignity are not easy to come by. Ask God to clothe you today with all that is necessary to face what (only He knows) is coming your way. Take time to list the pieces of the armor of God and thank Him for providing it to conquer all that today holds for you.

_____

_____

_____

_____

_____

_____

_____

_____

_____

_____

_____

_____

_____

_____

_____

_____

_____

_____

_____

_____

_____

Today's Meal
Hot Ham and Cheese Rolls

2 pkgs. Hawaiian rolls
Topping: 1 stick butter
1 lb. Münster cheese
1 t. poppy seeds
2 lb. honey ham (shaved)
½ T. Worcestershire sauce
2 t. minced onion
1 T. mustard

Slice each package of rolls lengthwise. Place bottoms of rolls in 10.5x14.75-inch baking dish (or divide into two 9x13-inch pans). Layer half of the cheese, all the ham, and then the other half of the cheese. Cover with tops of rolls.

Melt butter and add other topping ingredients. Brush over rolls, making sure to spread seeds and onions evenly. Cover and bake at 350° for 25 minutes. Uncover and bake for an additional 5–10 minutes until lightly toasted.

These are a favorite no matter where they go, but feel free to halve the recipe if only for your family.

Just in Case

Strength and dignity are her clothing, and she laughs at the time to come.

Proverbs 31:25

BEING DRESSED WITH STRENGTH AND DIGNITY IS PART OF DAILY PREPARATION. SOMETIMES WE need to be reminded of the strength that is ours through Christ on a moment-by-moment basis throughout our day. This is not a feeling. It is a fact that we must know and believe. If you wait until you "feel" strong you will likely find yourself ill prepared for your situation. For a gentle reminder, you can go back and reread yesterday's lesson, which encourages you to put on the full armor of God.

Today we will look at the second part of verse 25: "She laughs at the time to come." Why does she laugh? She is ready for whatever comes her way. Though Matthew was written hundreds of years later, our friend in Proverbs knew that anxiety about tomorrow was foolishness (Matthew 6:34). She was not only ready for what she knew she would face that day but she packed her bags and suited up with God's armor just in case.

In the physical world, we prepare for "just in case" as well. When we go on vacation, we prepare by packing extra clothes, bug spray, aloe vera for sunburns, umbrellas, etc., just in case. Then, when it clouds up at the amusement park and your family frets, you pull out your umbrella and rain ponchos. While everyone else is scrambling to get out of the weather, you laugh and carry on with business as usual. When pesky bugs are determined to ruin your camping trip, you break out the citronella and Skin So Soft. For every situation, you are prepared and laugh at whatever might come your way.

How beautiful it is to have God's Word in our hearts to use the exact same way.

> I have stored up your word in my heart, that I might not sin against
> you. (Psalm 119:11)

Isn't this exactly what Jesus did when He was tempted? With God's Word in our hearts, we are prepared for anything Satan tries to throw at us and we can laugh in his face!

Reflection and Application

1. How well do you have God's Word stored in your heart (on a scale of 1 to 10)? What is your plan for increasing this number?

2. What key verses do you have memorized that help you through the day? If you cannot think of any, look up a few that would be of help in the near future.

3. What are your current anxieties about tomorrow?

4. Read 1 Peter 5:6–7. Look at your answer to question number 3. Write your list again, and beside each statement write a verse that speaks truth into that situation as you cast it upon your Savior, who has already taken care of it.

5. Write Psalm 119:11 on an index card and place it in a prominent place in your home.

6. Choose a verse in the Bible that you and your family can memorize together this week. Help them hide it in their hearts. Write the verse and reference below.

Prayer/Journal

Ask God to give you a hunger for His Word. Ask Him for guidance in memorizing Scripture that you need to hide in your heart so you can laugh at the time to come. Share this prayer from Deuteronomy 6:4–9 with your family, and work on this together.

_____

_____

_____

_____

_____

_____

_____

_____

_____

_____

_____

_____

_____

_____

_____

_____

_____

_____

_____

Today's Meal
Chicken Flautas, Guacamole

4–5 chicken breasts (boiled and shredded)
  or shredded rotisserie chicken
3 Roma tomatoes
2–3 T. extra virgin olive oil
2 lg. garlic cloves
1 med. onion
Salt to taste
2 jalapenos
½ c. chicken broth
Corn tortillas
Oil for frying

Slice veggies in half (lengthwise). Drizzle griddle with olive oil. Place veggies cut side down on hot griddle. Cook veggies until they begin to brown; turn over. Place veggies in a blender and blend until liquified. Pour sauce into skillet and simmer. Add chicken broth and salt to taste.

Roll shredded chicken in warm corn tortillas and secure with toothpicks, or secure 3 at a time with wooden skewers.

Heat oil in medium skillet to 350°. Place rolled chicken in oil and fry until crispy but not too brown.

Top flautas with sauce, lettuce, tomato, onion, and crema as desired.

See guacamole recipe on page 46.

Words of the Wise

She opens her mouth with wisdom,
and the teaching of kindness is on her tongue.

Proverbs 31:26

WE LEARN FROM THE WOMAN WE'VE BEEN STUDYING THAT NOT ONLY DO HER ACTIONS AND work honor the Lord, but when she opens her mouth, wisdom and kindness flow. This woman honors Him in word and deed. But where does she get her wisdom? How does she know just the right thing to say to brighten someone's day, to encourage another's heart, or to lift someone's spirit? My best guess is that she has learned from experience and from mistakes (yes, she makes them too), but mostly she learns straight from God Himself.

God teaches us by His Spirit in us and through us. James, the half brother of Jesus, teaches us that God gives us wisdom when we ask in faith. Then He gives us the power to speak it when we understand the necessity of taming the tongue. With God's wisdom and the willingness to let Him tame our tongues, we too can open our mouths with words of wisdom and kindness. As time permits, read chapters 1–3 of James this week. Be prepared. This one always hits me where it hurts, as I make a living with words. Satan loves nothing more than to destroy what God has planned through what I speak and write. Satan wants to twist your words as well. Beware and remember Paul's exhortation:

> Let no corrupting talk come out of your mouths, but only such as is
> good for building up, as it fits the occasion, that it may give grace to
> those who hear. (Ephesians 4:29)

Words of wisdom and kindness do not come naturally to our human hearts, nor from our mouths. But with the help of God, He blesses us with the wisdom and ability to love our neighbor and speak words of grace.

Reflection and Application

1. In what ways do you relate to the rare and unique wisdom found in today's message?

2. What would it look like to place the filter of God's love over your mouth so that others hear blessings from Him?

3. Write down some words of grace that someone recently said to you.

4. Read Psalm 141:3. What does God need to guard against coming from your mouth?

5. Read Luke 6:45. What is in your heart? What is overflowing? List below what may be causing words that are negative or hurtful.

6. What words of wisdom and kindness do you have to share? Write down at least one person's name and the kind words of wisdom you have for them. (Be sensitive to the Lord and let Him guide you.)

Prayer / Journal

Pray about your response to question number 6. Pray for the person(s) you listed and then pray about how you can lift them up with words of kindness and wisdom.

_____

_____

_____

_____

_____

_____

_____

_____

_____

_____

_____

_____

_____

_____

_____

_____

_____

_____

Today's Meal
Buffalo Chicken Grilled Cheese

Two slices of bread
2–3 T. buffalo wing sauce
Butter
2 slices provolone cheese
¼–½ c. shredded rotisserie chicken
Combine chicken with sauce.

Butter one side of each piece of bread and place on a hot griddle. Once the butter is slightly melted, flip each piece of bread and allow that side to toast. Once toasted, reduce the heat to medium. Flip one slice of bread and layer it with one slice of cheese, sauced chicken, and another slice of cheese. Then top with the other piece of bread, buttered side up. Flip the sandwich when the bottom is toasted. Remove from the heat when cheese is melted and bottom piece of bread is toasted as desired.

Enjoy with potato chips and ranch dip.

Be a Blessing
Weekend Wrap-Up

Using what you learned this week and the verses listed beside each statement, fill in the blanks to remind you of God's work in you as well as the work to which you have been called.

Hospitality 101: Understanding His Blessings

- God _____ us in Christ with every _____ blessing (Ephesians 1:3).

- God _____ our allotted time and our _____ place (Acts 17:26).

- All Scripture is _____ by God and is _____ (2 Timothy 3:16).

- God _____ the birds and _____ the lilies (Matthew 6:26–29).

- God gives _____ generously (James 1:5).

Hospitality 102: We Are a Blessing

- We are to be a _____ to our _____ (Proverbs 12:4).

- We _____ our neighbor as _____ (Matthew 19:19).

- We are _____ and _____ for every _____ work (2 Timothy 3:17).

- We should _____ God's Word in our _____ (Psalm 119:11).

- Our words should give _____ to all who _____ (Ephesians 4:29).

My thoughts concerning this week's study:

_____

_____

_____

_____

_____

_____

_____

_____

_____

_____

_____

_____

_____

_____

_____

_____

_____

_____

_____

_____

_____

_____

Weekend Wrap-Up Desserts

SIMPLE BERRY COBBLER

1 stick butter (melted)
1 c. whole milk
1 c. sugar (for cobbler)
2 c. berries or peaches (any kind, fresh or frozen)
1 c. self-rising flour
¼ c. sugar (for topping)

Preheat oven to 350˚. Grease 9x9-inch baking dish. In a medium mixing bowl, combine flour and sugar. Whisk in milk, then melted butter. Rinse and dry berries if fresh. Pour batter into baking dish. Sprinkle berries evenly on top of batter. Top with ¼ cup sugar and bake for 50 minutes. Sprinkle with an additional couple of tablespoons of sugar, if desired, for crispy sugar crust on top. Bake for additional 10 minutes, regardless.

This is an awesome simple cobbler that is great with Cool Whip and/or ice cream. Enjoy!

BTW: My family loves fresh-picked blackberry the best.

ULTIMATE CAMP HOUSE COOKIES

1 can sweetened condensed milk
1 ½ c. flaked coconut
1 stick butter
1 c. white chocolate chips
1 ½ c. graham cracker crumbs
1 c. semisweet chocolate chips
2 t. baking powder
1 c. chopped pecans
½ c. flour

In a large bowl, mix sweetened condensed milk and butter at a low speed until smooth. In a separate bowl combine graham cracker crumbs, baking powder, and flour. Slowly add dry ingredients to milk mixture while continuing to mix on low. Stir in coconut, chocolate chips, and nuts by hand. Drop by tablespoon on ungreased baking stone. Bake at 375˚ for 10 minutes.

This is a great one to double and take on trips, camping, church functions, or to keep in the cookie jar.

If doubling, I just use the whole bag of chips and coconut instead of measuring them out. You can also substitute walnuts for pecans if you wish.

It works best with a stand mixer, as the batter gets really thick. Try not to eat it all before you actually bake them. LOL!

The table is set for your girly-girl meal.

Inner Beauty

While we regularly check ourselves out in the mirror to make adjustments to our outer physical appearance, how often do we look into the mirror of God's Word to do the same for our inner spiritual being? This week we will study what makes the Proverbs 31 woman beautiful. What makes her family rise each day to praise her with their actions and attitudes of respect and honor? She is a woman after God's own heart who humbly accepts her role in her household. We will also discover that inner beauty develops best when sharpened and encouraged by other beautiful women.

1 Peter 3:4: "But let your adorning be the hidden person of the heart with the imperishable beauty of a gentle and quiet spirit, which in God's sight is very precious." You are precious in His sight! You are **priceless**! So grab a girlfriend with whom you can study and pray this week.

Girls will be girls. We all have our favorite shops and boutiques that just will not suit the men in our lives. Women are uniquely wired for relationship with one another. We lift one another up. We laugh together, cry together, and shop together. But no ladies' day or night out is complete without a good meal together. When it is just us girls, we choose food and venues that are particularly designed to our tastes. Women love to get together for finger sandwiches and tea. Men? Not so much. This week's recipes are just for women and are most commonly designed for the girly-girl in all of us. So skip the café and invite the ladies to your home. You will all be blessed when you do.

Daddy, thank You for making me a woman. Help me to be a woman after Your own heart. Lead me as I build relationships with other women. Help me be a mentor to those who look up to me, and lead me to someone who will encourage and strengthen me in my walk with You. I long to have relationships that honor You. Show me how to love and serve as You would.

Amen.

Women are uniquely wired for
relationship with one another.
We lift one another up.
We laugh together,
cry together, and shop together.

Her Home

She looks well to the ways of her household
and does not eat the bread of idleness.

Proverbs 31:27

FHA: Future Homemakers of America. Home economics is not really taught in schools anymore. At least, it isn't taught the way I had it in high school. We learned how to cook, sew, clean, shop, and budget. I still use and share some of the recipes that I learned in class twenty-five-plus years ago. One of the most important things we learned in class was that taking care of a house is an honor, and that when it is done well, everyone who enters is blessed. In fact, after years of watching my mother take care of our house and all that I learned from Mrs. Nita Young in Home Ec., I realized that managing a house well is what makes it a home. Managing the budget, groceries, children, and cleaning were only part of the equation. These women showed me by example that, while all of this may be done impeccably, in order to have real hospitality, we must have the attitude and mind of Christ.

> Let love be genuine. Abhor what is evil; hold fast to what is good. Love one another with brotherly affection. Outdo one another in showing honor. Do not be slothful in zeal, be fervent in spirit, serve the Lord. Rejoice in hope, be patient in tribulation, be constant in prayer. Contribute to the needs of the saints and seek to show hospitality. (Romans 12:9–13)

What is hospitality?

The dictionary defines hospitality as being cordial and generous to guests. You have read in weeks past that it really goes deeper than this dictionary definition. Genuine hospitality is opening your heart to share and receive from others—touching someone else's heart with a piece of your own. It involves genuine love (v. 9), brotherly affection, and showing honor (v. 10). This is inner beauty. This is what makes your house a home, no matter how clean it is or how gourmet the meal.

Reflection and Application

1. What is it about your home that makes everyone love walking in the door?

2. What is your definition of hospitality?

3. Real hospitality is rare. How and when are you hospitable to others?

4. Read the passage from Romans in today's devotion. Underline each of the "do" commands. Circle the "do not" command.

5. Write the commands that may be more difficult for you.

6. Check your calendar, talk to your family, and schedule a dinner date with at least one other couple or family in the next month. Write some dinner and entertainment ideas.

Prayer/Journal

Pray and ask God to show you how to make your house a home and a safe place for your family to live and for others to visit. Ask God who needs to know His heart of hospitality and for Him to use you to show that person His steadfast, unconditional love.

_____

_____

_____

_____

_____

_____

_____

_____

_____

_____

_____

_____

_____

_____

_____

_____

_____

_____

_____

_____

Today's Meal
Hot Chicken Salad

4–5 chicken breasts (cooked and shredded)
4 T. lemon juice
2 cans cream of chicken soup
Salt and pepper to taste
1 c. real mayonnaise
2 c. grated cheddar cheese
4 T. minced onion
2–3 c. crushed potato chips
3 c. celery (chopped finely)

Mix all ingredients except cheese and potato chips in a 9x13-inch baking dish. Top with cheese and chips. Bake at 350° for 30–35 minutes.

This salad is good on crackers or sandwiches. It is also great as a dip with sturdy chips.

I have also served it in phyllo dough mini cups. This makes a great bite-sized appetizer. Spoon mixture into mini cups instead of baking dish and bake for half the time.

Blessed

Her children rise up and call her blessed; her husband also, and he praises her.

Proverbs 31:28

HAPPY. REVERED. CONSECRATED. SACRED. SANCTIFIED. ALL OF THESE WORDS ARE SYNONYMOUS with the word blessed. So why do her children rise up and call her blessed? Because she has invested her life into theirs, her family considers her worthy of praise. She is a blessing to her family and her community.

Would your family call you blessed? Does your husband find you praiseworthy? Whether or not they voice it, you are! I understand that many of our tasks are thankless ones. A lot of what we do every day goes unrecognized and seemingly unappreciated.

God sees! He knows!
He cares! He blesses!

However, your children will one day (when they have families of their own) realize all that you do and will rise up and call you blessed. And, just as a tag to this thought, God sees! He knows! He cares! He blesses!

When we read the Beatitudes in Matthew 5, we see a whole list of those who are blessed: those who are poor in spirit, meek, merciful, pure in heart, peacemakers, persecuted for righteousness' sake, reviled, and those who mourn and hunger and thirst for righteousness. Wow, what a list! When it comes to family and raising children, we probably fit many of these categories, and at times, all at once. Jesus Himself calls us blessed. Blessed when we make peace in our homes; blessed when we show mercy instead of acting in anger; blessed when we hunger and thirst for what is right in our homes and in the lives of our children; blessed when we are persecuted for being the only parents who say no.

Rejoice and be glad, for your reward is great in heaven.
(Matthew 5:12)

You are blessed, my friend. God has sanctified you and set you apart. The consecration we receive from God on the inside is displayed as blessings to others as we live in thanksgiving and joy.

Reflection and Application

1. When was the last time you felt as though you were blessed? Write a brief description below.

2. How can you specifically bless someone in your home today?

3. How can you be a blessing to someone in your community today?

4. Look up the definition of blessed in your dictionary or on your phone. Write down the words that apply to you.

5. Read Matthew 5:1–12. To which Beatitudes do you most relate? Do you see any correspondence between this answer and your answer to question number 4?

6. Why do you think hard times and struggles make us blessed?

Prayer / Journal

Thank God today for making you a blessing. Thank Him for setting you apart as blessed. Ask God who you can contact to tell them what a blessing they are to you.

_____

_____

_____

_____

_____

_____

_____

_____

_____

_____

_____

_____

_____

_____

_____

_____

_____

_____

_____

_____

_____

_____

_____

Today's Meal
Finger Sandwiches: Carrot Sandwiches, Cucumber Sandwiches

CARROT SANDWICHES

8 oz. cream cheese
1 tsp. garlic salt
½ pkg. Lipton onion soup mix
1–2 tsp. cayenne pepper
5 lg. carrots (chopped fine)
½ c. mayonnaise
1 c. pecans (chopped)
½ tsp. dehydrated garlic chips

Mix all ingredients and let chill. Spread on bread slices and make sandwiches.

For finger sandwiches, gently cut away crust with a bread knife. Slice sandwich into 4 finger sandwiches.

I understand this sounds like a strange combination and you may not even like carrots. Personally, I do not like carrots, but I love these sandwiches.

CUCUMBER SANDWICHES

1 lg. cucumber
8 oz. cream cheese
3 green onions (chopped)
Mayonnaise to taste
Garlic powder

Shred the cucumber with cheese grater and allow it to drain on a paper towel until most of the liquid is absorbed. Mix the cream cheese and small amount of mayo until smooth and spreadable. Stir in onions and garlic powder. Add cucumber and mix well.

Follow finger-sandwich directions above.

Surpassing Excellence

Many women have done excellently, but you surpass them all.

Proverbs 31:29

WE WORK AT BEING VIRTUOUS, EXCELLENT, AND STRONG. WE ACCOMPLISH THIS IN DIFFERENT ways as we are unique, rare, and beautiful. Don't let Satan try to throw you off and make you think that you are "less than." Today's verse is a quote from a husband to his wife. No matter what version of the Bible you read, Proverbs 31:28 ends with punctuation that indicates that the next words are the praises from her husband. Today we see the words that he says: "Many women have done excellently, but you surpass them all."

This husband knows his wife better than anyone else. She is his bride. She is his friend. She is his helper. He knows her strengths, weaknesses, gifts, and talents. He loves her more than his own life. He sees her as excellent. More than that, she surpasses excellence because of who she is to him.

> Husbands, love your wives, as Christ loved the church and gave him-
> self up for her, that he might sanctify her, having cleansed her by the
> washing of water with the word, so that he might present the church
> to himself in splendor, without spot or wrinkle or any such thing,
> that she might be holy and without blemish. (Ephesians 5:25–27)

Married or not, godly husband or not, you surpass excellence.

Jesus knows you better than anyone else. You are His bride (Ephesians 5). You are His friend (John 15:15). You are His helper (Matthew 25:40). He knows your strengths, weaknesses, gifts, and talents (Psalm 139:1–4). He loves you more than His own life (John 10:11). He sees you as excellent (Isaiah 1:18). More than that, you surpass excellence because of who you are in Him!

Though we may rarely hear praises from our families, we can always know who we are in Christ.

Reflection and Application

1.   Who knows you best? How likely are you to try to please that person over anyone else? Why?

2.   Do you see yourself as surpassing excellence? Why or why not?

3.   From the last paragraph in today's devotion, which characteristic of your relationship with Jesus is most difficult to grasp? Which one is easiest? Why?

4.   Praising God and others doesn't always come easy for us. Take time to thank God for the relationships in your life, and then contact someone special and let them know how much you appreciate their influence on your life.

5.   Read Psalm 139. Make notes below regarding your thoughts about how God knows and loves you.

6.   Get in front of a mirror and read the last paragraph aloud to yourself, changing the pronouns to make it personal: Jesus knows *me* better than anyone else. *I* am His bride . . .

Prayer/Journal

Thank God today for His excellence. Thank Him for His Son, Who died so that you can have His excellence inside of you. Ask Him how to live out excellence in the life He has planned for you.

_____

_____

_____

_____

_____

_____

_____

_____

_____

_____

_____

_____

_____

_____

_____

_____

_____

_____

Today's Meal
Cranberry Almond Chicken Salad

3–4 chicken breasts (cooked and diced)

¾ c. sliced almonds

1 ½ c. red grapes (sliced)

2 T. sugar

11 oz. mandarin oranges (drained and crushed)

1 c. Craisins

1 c. celery (chopped fine)

Sauce:

1 c. mayonnaise

3 t. soy sauce

3 t. lemon juice

Rehydrate Craisins by soaking them in a glass of water overnight or until plump. Drain. In a small skillet, place almonds and sugar. Over medium heat sauté until sugar is melted and almonds are golden brown. Remove from heat and pour onto nonstick surface to cool.

In a medium mixing bowl combine chicken, sliced grapes, oranges, celery, almonds and rehydrated Craisins. In a small bowl, mix sauce ingredients. Pour over chicken mixture, stir well, and let chill.

This is best served on fresh croissants as a sandwich. I like to put the sandwich together and press it in the panini press of my George Foreman Grill.

Serve with kettle-cooked potato chips.

A Woman Who Fears the Lord

> Charm is deceitful, and beauty is vain,
> but a woman who fears the Lord is to be praised.
>
> Proverbs 31:30

WHO ARE WE TRYING TO IMPRESS? MAN, THE MIRROR, OR OUR GOD? FROM WHERE DOES OUR beauty come? Our closet, our cosmetics, or our fear of the Lord? Whose beauty does the world see? Ours or our God's? This quandary seems to rear its head often when I know that I am about to make a first impression or when I feel as though I must fix a less-than-desirable first impression. Satan tries his best to accuse and discourage us in our weakest places. Many times, for women, it is in the area of self-image.

This quote from author Sam Levenson in *One Era and Out the Other: A Life's Journey* sheds some light on our dilemma and, once again, offers some perspective.

> For attractive lips, speak words of kindness. For lovely eyes, seek out the good in people. For a slim figure, share your food with the hungry. For beautiful hair, let a child run their fingers through it once a day. For poise, walk with the knowledge that you never walk alone. People, more than things, have to be restored, renewed, revived, reclaimed, and redeemed. Remember, if you ever need a helping hand, you will find one at the end of each of your arms. As you grow older, you will discover that you have two hands, one for helping yourself and the other for helping others. (Pocket Books, 1974, p. 177)

Sam wrote this poem, "Time Tested Beauty Tips," for his grandchild. I do not know where he stood in regard to his faith, but he got it right.

> But let your adorning be the hidden person of the heart with the imperishable beauty of a gentle and quiet spirit, which in God's sight is very precious. (1 Peter 3:4)

If we spend more time in the mirror of God's Word and let it mold us into His image, we'll spend a lot less time in front of our physical mirrors trying to cover and change our outer appearance.

Reflection and Application

1. If you could change one thing about your physical appearance, what would it be? Why?

2. Read Mr. Levenson's poem again. What strikes you the most about the beauty described?

3. Based on 1 Peter 3:4 and the poem combined, what beauty tip do you take away as something new and/or challenging?

4. Write your own definition of what it means to "fear the Lord."

5. Search the book of Proverbs and list three Scriptures that use the phrase "fear the Lord."

6. Using your answers to question number 5, record below what challenges you the most about living your life in the "fear of the Lord."

Prayer / Journal

You are beautiful! Thank God for the way He made you. Write Psalm 139:14, word for word, in today's prayer, and then write it in your own words.

_____

_____

_____

_____

_____

_____

_____

_____

_____

_____

_____

_____

_____

_____

_____

_____

_____

_____

_____

Today's Meal
Chicken Penne Pasta

This is excellent all by itself. However, if you have hearty eaters, serve with garlic bread and salad on the side.

Drizzle of olive oil
Salt and pepper to taste
4 cloves garlic
¼ c. fresh basil leaves
2 c. cherry tomatoes
2 oz. parmesan cheese
3 c. penne pasta
2 c. grilled and shredded chicken breasts
3 c. chicken broth

In a 3-quart pot, drizzle olive oil. Thinly slice garlic and add to pot with whole tomatoes. Over medium heat, cover and allow to cook 2 minutes. When tomatoes are tender enough to pop with a fork, mash them. Add chicken broth, pasta, salt and pepper. Increase heat to high and let boil until pasta is tender. Coarsely chop basil and grate cheese. Add chicken, ¾ cup basil, and parmesan to the pot and stir. Garnish with remaining basil and extra cheese as desired.

Her Reward

Give her the fruit of her hands, and let her works praise her in the gates.

Proverbs 31:31

How wonderfully tasty are summer vegetables from your garden. They are the best because they are the fruit of your labor. Somehow there seems to be more flavor and richness from the joy of knowing it comes as a result of your sweat and effort. If you do not have a garden, as I do not, you most likely appreciate fresh vegetables from generous friends and family members who do. Or, at the very least, you relish in the summer produce from nearby farmers' markets.

Today we celebrate! We celebrate the return for our work. We have examined and discussed all that Proverbs 31 suggests are the qualities of a virtuous woman. It is no wonder after all we have learned in these six weeks that she is hard to find. Yet we know deep down she is inside each one of us. As women who fear the Lord, we celebrate as we watch our children grow. We celebrate as our husbands are well known and respected. We celebrate as our communities are well served. And we celebrate because of the inner beauty provided by our Lord. As women who fear the Lord, we celebrate as our work is rewarded and we will one day hear these precious words:

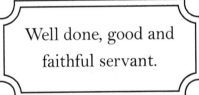

Well done, good and faithful servant.

"Well done, good and faithful servant. You have been faithful over little; I will set you over much. Enter into the joy of your master." (Matthew 25:21)

Read all of Proverbs 31 from *The Message* today. Look for yourself in the midst of the text. After studying for six weeks, you'll be surprised how much you have in common with the ideal woman and how blessed you are because of your efforts.

You are fearfully and wonderfully made! Well done, good and faithful servant. Come, you who are blessed by the Father, inherit the kingdom prepared for you from the foundation of the world.

Reflection and Application

1. What have you learned about Proverbs 31 that you did not know before reading this book?

2. Have you come to see yourself as priceless? Explain how.

3. What are your next steps toward hospitality?

4. Read Matthew 25:31–41. How does this text align with Proverbs 31?

5. Go back and read the Weekend Wrap-Up pages from each week. Which principles of hospitality have you mastered?

6. Which principles of hospitality is God still teaching you?

Prayer / Journal

I thank God for you. I have prayed for each of you and will continue to do so. Thank Him today for all that He has taught you. Make notes on lessons you still need to review. Ask God to help you as you grow in the fear of the Lord, walk in priceless freedom, and practice the principles of hospitality.

_____

_____

_____

_____

_____

_____

_____

_____

_____

_____

_____

_____

_____

_____

_____

_____

_____

_____

_____

_____

_____

Today's Meal
Greek Tortellini Salad

Salad:
20 oz. pkg. refrigerated tortellini
1 lg. cucumber, chopped
1 c. black olives, sliced
1 c. grape tomatoes, halved
½ red onion, chopped
¾ c. feta cheese, crumbled
2 c. chicken breast, cooked and cubed (optional)

Dressing:
¼ c. extra virgin olive oil
3 T. red wine vinegar
1 clove garlic, minced
½ t. oregano
Salt and pepper to taste

Cook tortellini according to package directions. Strain and rinse in cool water. Set aside. In a large bowl combine tomatoes, chopped cucumber, olives, onion, cheese, and chicken breast. In a small bowl, whisk dressing. Pour over salad and toss well. Add tortellini and gently combine.

Chill for at least one hour.

This makes a whole lot! Make it for a ladies' brunch or potluck. The critics will rave!

Inner Beauty
Weekend Wrap-Up

Using what you learned this week and the verses listed beside each statement, fill in the blanks to remind you of God's beauty and the beauty He created in you for the benefit of others.

Hospitality 101: Understanding His Beauty

- The _____ _____ is the good _____ entrusted to us (2 Timothy 1:14).

- From God we receive an _____ which is our _____ (Colossians 3:24).

- God _____ and _____ us (Psalm 139:1).

- God is the _____ of _____ (Psalm 50:2).

- He is the _____. Without Him, we can do _____ (John 15:5).

Hospitality 102: Our Inner Beauty

- We should seek to show genuine _____ (Romans 12:13).

- We _____ for our _____ is in _____ (Matthew 5:12).

- We _____ because He _____ loved us (1 John 4:19).

- We let our _____ be the _____ person of the heart (1 Peter 3:4).

- When we _____ much _____. God is _____ (John 15:8).

My thoughts concerning this week's study:

_____

_____

_____

_____

_____

_____

_____

_____

_____

_____

_____

_____

_____

_____

_____

_____

_____

_____

_____

_____

_____

Weekend Wrap-Up Desserts

STRAWBERRY POUND CAKE TRIFLE

This is a beautiful dish. It is simple and inexpensive, yet sells well in bake sales and auctions. Enjoy!

1 lb. frozen pound cake (Sara Lee)
2 pt. strawberries (sliced)
1 lg. pkg. cheesecake-flavored instant pudding
   (made by pkg directions)
1 lg. tub Cool Whip

Dice pound cake into 1-inch cubes. Layer cake on bottom of a trifle bowl. Layer pudding next, then strawberries and Cool Whip. Repeat until you run out of ingredients or until you reach the top of your bowl, ending with Cool Whip. Garnish with extra strawberries. Chill for 1 hour.

FRUIT PIZZA

This recipe without the fruit is my take on Bavarian cream pizza. Try it with or without the fruit. You won't be disappointed.

1 lg. pkg. sugar cookie dough
8 oz. cream cheese
½ c. powdered sugar
¾ c. yellow cake mix
½ stick butter (melted)
Fruit of your choice

Press sugar cookie dough onto round pizza stone or round baking sheet. Mix cream cheese with powdered sugar until smooth. Spread over cookie dough, leaving ¼-inch edges. Sprinkle cake mix over surface of cream cheese. Pour melted butter over the top. Bake at 350° for 10–12 minutes. Allow to cool and top with your favorite fruit or serve by itself.

Index

Main Dishes

Side Dishes

Desserts

Almond Joy Pie, 31
Chocolate Chip Cookies, 31
Chocolate Pie, 31
Coconut Pie, 31
Crème Brûlée, 57
Darn-Good Pies, 109
Dump Cake, 83

Fruit Pizza, 161
Homemade Crunchy Caramel Candy Bars, 109
Shortbread, 57
Simple Berry Cobbler, 135
Strawberry Pound Cake Trifle, 161
Strawberry Surprise, 83
Ultimate Camp House Cookies, 135

Order Information

To order additional copies of this book, please visit
www.redemption-press.com.
Also available on Amazon.com and BarnesandNoble.com
Or by calling toll free 1-844-2REDEEM.